The Questions _and_ Answers BOOK

for the

Private Pilots Licence

Jim Stevens and Jeremy M. Pratt

Aviation Law

Meteorology

Navigation

Aircraft General

Human Performance and Limitations

Radiotelephony

First Edition 1993
Second Edition 1994

The Questions and Answers Book
for the Private Pilots Licence

Jim Stevens & Jeremy M Pratt

ISBN 1-874783-55-1

Published by:

AIRPLAN FLIGHT EQUIPMENT

Southside, Manchester International Airport, Wilmslow, Cheshire, SK9 4LL, UK
Tel: 0161-499 0023   Fax: 0161-499 0298

Acknowledgments

We would like to thank the following for their help and advice:

AOPA

Adrian Dickinson

Steve Dickinson

Ron Campbell

Premo Lonzardi

Medway Flight Training

David Ogilvy

Martin Robinson

Ian Sixsmith

Rob Taylor - GDi studio

Section Contents

CONDUCT OF THE EXAMINATION

The examination usually takes place at the Flying Training Organisation (FTO) under the supervision of a CAA authorised examiner.

Candidates are expected to provide their own navigation, writing & calculating equipment. Reference books, notes and electronic calculators are **not** permitted. The exam room will have any relevant posters or publications removed. The candidate would not normally be expected to leave and re-enter the exam room whilst the examination is in progress; so go to the toilet first!

Each exam has a specified time limit which will be strictly observed. The person supervising the exam is not allowed to discuss the examination, interpretation of questions etc. whilst the examination is in progress. The exam question paper should not be marked in any way. Use the back of the answer sheet for any rough workings you want to do.

Once the exam is finished, the authorised examiner will mark the paper. In the event of a pass the examiner will discuss any questions wrongly answered. In the event of a fail, the examiner may indicate general areas of weakness, but will not discuss answers to specific questions.

There are three examination papers for each subject, it is not permitted to take the same paper twice. Should the candidate fail all three papers, arrangements will be made for an examination by a CAA staff examiner.

The candidate should be warned before the exam starts that any infringement of the rules will result in disqualification.

EXAMINATION TECHNIQUE

All the examinations are of the multiple choice type - marks are **not** deducted for an incorrect answer.

Before starting the exam paper read through the instructions carefully. Check the time limit so that you know when the exam will finish.

Unless there are specific instructions otherwise, tackle the questions you are sure you can answer first, and return to difficult questions later. Read each question carefully and be sure you understand exactly what is being asked. There will be only one correct answer, sometimes you can reach this by eliminating the wrong answers.

You are not allowed spare paper, or to mark the examination paper in any way. Do any workings out on the back of the answer sheet.

Generally the exams are not 'time - pressure' type, so you may well finish the paper before the time limit is reached. If this is the case the remaining time is best spent by re-checking the answers you have given. Re-read each question carefully to be sure you have understood it properly and have given the correct answer. Remember that marks are not deducted for an incorrect answer, so if you really cannot select the correct answer for a question it is worth taking a guess.

Although good examination technique will help you make the best of your knowledge, it does not guarantee a pass. The best preparation for the exam is to learn the subject fully. Your FTO will not enter you for an exam unless they feel you know the subject well enough to have a good chance of passing. Even once you have passed an exam, you cannot assume that your knowledge of that subject is complete. You should regularly revise and update each subject to keep your knowledge current.

USE OF THIS PUBLICATION

To get the best out of this publication you should tackle each paper in order. After completing a paper mark your answers to assess your result. Review any questions you answered incorrectly to see if there is an area in which your knowledge is weak. If this is the case revise that area before attempting the next paper.

It must be stressed that you should review the whole of an area in which you are failing questions. This publication has been designed to test your complete knowledge of each subject area. It is not possible to pass the exam by learning set answers to set questions.

Initially the time limit should be taken as a guide only. In later papers you should aim to be obtaining a pass mark within the specified time limit.

Remember the surest way to pass the exam is to know the subject thoroughly!

Instructions

1   Time allowed 30 minutes.

2   Twenty multi-choice questions each carrying 5 marks. Marks are not deducted for wrong answers. The pass mark is 70%.

3   Unless otherwise indicated, the questions relate to a British registered aircraft or an aircraft operating in British airspace.

4   Read each question carefully as there is only one answer which is correct.

5   Remember examination technique, you are advised to pass over questions that seem difficult at first sight and return to them when you have answered the others.

Note:

Unless otherwise specified, the questions relate to a UK licenced pilot, operating a UK registered aircraft in UK airspace.

1 For what period of time is the UK PPL valid?

A 13 months

B 10 years

C Life

2 For a UK PPL to be valid the licence must include a current:

A Certificate of Experience.

B Certificate of Test, Certificate of Experience, and medical.

C Certificate of Test or Certificate of Experience, and medical.

3 A marshaller holding his left arm down and moving the right repeatedly upward and backward means:

A Open up the port engine or turn to starboard.

B Open up the starboard engine or turn to port.

C Proceed to the marshaller on this marshallers right.

4 In relation to flight over a congested area, an aircraft may not:

A Fly below 3000'.

B Perform aerobatics.

C Practice an engine failure.

5 A "Group A" licence entitles the holder to act as PIC on:

A All single engined aeroplanes not exceeding 5700 kg MTWA.

B All aeroplanes not exceeding 5700 kg MTWA.

C All single engined aeroplanes not exceeding 2300 kg MTWA.

6 The pilot of a Cessna 172 is planning a flight from Liverpool to Dublin. Assuming the flight in made under VFR, which of the following is correct?

A The pilot has the option of filing a full flight plan because the flight will be over water.

B The pilot must file a full flight plan, not less than 60 minutes before requesting taxy

C The pilot must file a full flight plan, not less than 30 minutes before requesting taxy.

7 Except where otherwise notified, the holder of a PPL without any instrument qualifications may fly on a SVFR clearance in a control zone NOT notified for schedule 8 of the ANO subject to a minimum flight visibility of:

A 5km

B 8km

C 10km

8 To operate an aircraft radio, a radiotelephony licence must be held:

A And renewed every 12 months.

B Except for a student pilot in the course of his/her training.

C Except by the holder of a valid PPL

9 Approaching an aerodrome non-radio, you receive a flashing red light from the control tower. This means:

A Give way to other aircraft and continue circling.

B Do not land; wait for permission to land.

C Do not land; aerodrome not available for landing.

10 On a navigation exercise you become lost and are unable to contact an ATSU. You should:

A Dial 121.5 MHz and make a MAYDAY call.

B Dial 121.5 MHz and make a PAN PAN call.

C Begin circling and wait for assistance.

11 Having consumed alcohol at 2300 hrs on 23/5, you are advised not to fly before:

A 0700 hrs 24/5

B 2300 hrs 24/5

C 2300 hrs 30/5

12 A white T in the signal area means:

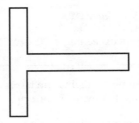

A Aeroplanes and gliders taking off or landing must do so parallel with the shaft of the T and towards the cross arm.

B The aerodrome has technical facilities for aircraft engineering.

C Approach and take off is particularly susceptible to turbulence.

13 If a marshaller wishes you to STOP, which of the following is the correct action:

A Arms repeatedly crossed above the head. The speed of arm movement indicates the urgency of the stop.

B Arms placed above the head in a vertical position.

C Arms placed down and crossed in front of the body.

14 A PPL plans a flight outside controlled airspace that will have a cruising level of FL110. What specific items of equipment should be carried?

A A transponder and oxygen equipment.

B Oxygen equipment and a second altimeter

C A transponder and a two-way radio.

15 You see a series of projectiles fired from the ground at 10 second intervals, showing red and green stars. This indicates you are:

A In a MATZ.

B Over a firing range.

C In a Danger Area.

16 You are flying on a north easterly track and your MSA for that leg is 3100ft. You should fly at:

A 3100 ft QNH.

B 5000 ft QNH.

C FL50.

17 You must not fly within an active ATZ unless the commander has permission from ATC:

A Except if the aircraft is non-radio.

B Except when contact with the ground station cannot be made.

C Under any circumstances.

18 Green flashes directed at an aircraft in the air, from ATC, mean:

A You may land.

B Return to aerodrome, wait for permission to land.

C Land at this aerodrome after receiving continuous green light.

19 An aircraft must not fly over an open air gathering of 1000 people or more:

A Below 500 ft.

B Below 1500 ft within 2000 ft of the highest obstacle.

C Within 3000 ft.

20 When an aircraft is sighted, and you have right of way, you should maintain:

A Height, course and speed.

B Course and speed, and descend.

C Height and speed.

1 If flying more than 10 nm out to sea from the coast, a flight plan:

A Must be filed.

B Should be filed.

C Need not be filed.

2 Following an engine failure and successful forced   landing, you require medical help. To aid search and rescue you should lay out a visual signal in the shape of a letter. Which letter?

A X

B V

C M

3 Flying above the transition altitude, you should work out your cruising level from:

A Heading (True)

B Track (True)

C Track (Magnetic)

4 An accident must be reported if:

A At any time a person is killed on an aircraft.

B A wing tip is dented whilst taxying with people on board with the intention of flying.

C The commander of the aircraft spills his coffee.

5 A log book must be retained for what period after the last entry therein?

A 5 years

B 24 months

C 1 year

6 What transponder code should you use in the event of a radio failure?

A 7000

B 7500

C 7600

7 You are in an aircraft on the ground ready to take-off and see an aircraft on final approach. The air-ground radio instructs you, "cleared to immediate take-off". Do you;-

A Line up and take-off immediately, if you are satisfied it is safe to do so.

B Wait for the aircraft on final approach to land, then line up and wait.

C Ask the air traffic controller if he is aware of the aircraft on final approach.

8 In flight, in order to overtake a slower aircraft, you should:

A Climb above the other aircraft, and the other aircraft has priority.

B Overtake to the right, and you have priority.

C Overtake to the right, and the other aircraft has priority.

9 A marshaller holding his right arm down and repeatedly moving his left arm upward and backward means:

A Open up the starboard engine.

B Turn to port.

C Both A and B.

10 Generally, when flying on Instrument Flight Rules (IFR) above 3000' AMSL the minimum obstacle clearance is:

A 500 ft above the highest obstacle within 5nm.

B 1000 ft above the highest obstacle within 5nm.

C 1500 ft above the highest obstacle within 5nm.

11 If a dumb-bell displayed in the aerodrome signals area has a red letter L superimposed it means:

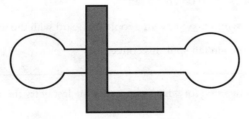

A Light aircraft must not proceed on the area marked with a white L.

B Light aircraft are allowed to take-off and land either on a runway or on the area designated by the white L.

C Light aircraft must only land on the area designated by a red L.

12 One provision of the low flying rules (rule 5) is a requirement to fly not less than 1500' above the highest fixed object within 2000'. An exemption to this provision is:

A Taking off and landing at any aerodrome.

B Taking off and landing at a licenced aerodrome.

C Whilst performing aerobatics.

13 At a civilian aerodrome, identification beacons flash two letter morse groups:

A Green, every 10 seconds.

B Green, every 12 seconds.

C Green, every 15 seconds.

14 You are about to release the brakes on the aircraft. What signal should you give to the marshaller?

A Raise arm and hand with fingers extended horizontally in front of face, then clench fist.

B Hands crossed in front of face, palms facing outwards, move arms outwards.

C Raise arm with fist clenched horizontally in front of face, then extend fingers.

---

15 You are looking for information on operational matters such as ATC services and requirements. What colour paper would it be if you were using AICs?

A White

B Yellow

C Green

---

16 Taxing to the hold before entering the active runway, you see several sets of markings. Which do you stop at?

A A solid yellow line.

B A ladder-style marking in yellow.

C Two continuous, and two broken lines in yellow.

---

17 With a PPL, you are not permitted to do any:

A Public Transport

B Glider towing.

C Parachute dropping.

---

18 An obstacle which is 310 feet above ground level:

A is in the UK AIP, and may be lit.

B is in the UK AIP, and must be lit.

C is not in the UK AIP, and should be lit.

---

19 The size of a Military Air Traffic Zone is:

A 3000 ft agl within a radius of 5nm from the midpoint of the longest runway, with stubs 4nm wide.

B 3000 ft amsl within a radius of 5nm from the midpoint of the aerodrome reference point, with stubs 4nm wide.

C 3000 ft agl within a radius of 2nm from the midpoint of the longest runway.

---

20 The semi-circular rule applies:

A at and above FL245.

B above FL245.

C at and above 24,500 ft. QNH

1 Which of the following information given by an ATC unit must you confirm by repeating it when acknowledging the message?

A Transponder code you are to squawk.

B Details of the weather.

C Direction and distance information passed to you about conflicting traffic.

2 A continuous green light directed from ATC to an aircraft in the air means:

A Return to aerodrome, wait for permission to land.

B You may land.

C After landing, vacate the runway and taxi to the apron.

3 With regard to the Air Navigation (General) Regulations, a pilot could carry out which of the following in certain circumstances:

A Replacement of safety belts or safety harnesses.

B Rib stitching of fabric not covering a control surface.

C Replacement of a landing wheel unit.

4 Whilst maintaining a steady course and altitude you spot another aircraft in your 2 o'clock at a range of 5nm. The other aircraft is at the same altitude as yourself. A real danger of collision exists if:

A the other aircraft appears to be moving into your twelve o'clock position.

B it appears to be stationary in relation to yourself.

C the other aircraft appears to be moving into your four o'clock position.

5 A marshaller moving his arms repeatedly upward and backward indicates:

A Move ahead.

B Lift off (Helicopter)

C Increase height of hover (Helicopters) for obstacle clearance.

6 During flight in an airliner, a person opens an over-head luggage locker, and is seriously injured by an object falling from it. Is this a reportable accident?

A Only the person injured was a member of the on-duty flight crew.

B No.

C Yes.

7 You see a rectangular red/yellow chequered board on the side of an ATC Tower. This means:

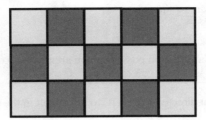

A   A right hand circuit is in force.

B   Aircraft may move on the manoeuvring area and apron only with the permission of ATC.

C   The area beyond this point is unfit for aircraft movement.

8 In the UK AIP, which of the following sections contains the contact frequency for an aerodrome?

A   GEN

B   AGA

C   COM

9 On flying machines and airships, the green and red lights show through _____ degrees from dead ahead. The white tail light shows through _____ degrees either side of dead astern. The missing numbers are:

A   110, 70

B   220, 140

C   100, 90

10 A marshaller making a circular motion of the right hand at head level, with the left arm pointing indicates:

A   Caution, helicopter hovering in the direction indicated.

B   Start the engine being pointed at.

C   Turn around and proceed in the direction the marshaller is pointing.

11 You see a fuel pump on an aerodrome painted red. This supplies:

A   AVGAS or AVTUR.

B   AVTUR or MOGAS.

C   MOGAS or AVGAS.

12 Which of the following is true?

A   Gliders must give way to airships and balloons.

B   Balloons must give way to airships.

C   Airships must give way to gliders and balloons.

13 An aircraft may not tow gliders unless:

A   The pilot has undergone instruction in glider towing.

B   It is permitted by the C of A.

C   The aircraft is insured for glider towing.

14 You are following a railway line north to south. To which side of the railway line should you fly?

A   East.

B   West.

C   East or West.

15 If illness persists, you should inform the authority in writing:

A   On the first day of illness.

B   On the twentieth day of illness.

C   On the twenty-first day of illness.

16 If you suffer injury affecting your capacity as flight crew:

A   You need not inform the CAA.

B   You must inform the CAA as soon as possible.

C   You should inform the CAA immediately.

17 If a required light fails in flight (other than an anti-collision light when flying by day) and cannot be repaired or replaced at once, the aircraft:

A   Should land as soon as is safe to do so unless ATC authorises continuation of the flight.

B   Must land at the next available aerodrome.

C   Can continue to its destination, and replace the faulty lights on arrival.

18 Should you inadvertently enter an area notified as restricted or prohibited, the actions are to:

A   continue on course, and try to make contact with the appropriate ATC.

B   to leave the area as quickly as possible, not descending whilst in the area.

C   to leave by the shortest route making height changes as is necessary for the continuation of your flight plan.

19 Transponder conspicuity code is?

A   7000

B   1215

C   1234

20 When is the only time that you turn to the left when approaching another moving aircraft?

A In the hangar

B In the air

C On the ground

1 Notams Class 1 are circulated by:

A Post

B Telephone

C AFTN

2 The standard ICAO abbreviation MEDA means:

A Minimum emergency distance available

B Maximum emergency distance available

C Military emergency diversion aerodrome

3 If you notice an error or omission in the AIP you should:

A Inform the AIDU

B Inform the CAA

C Do nothing

4 The standard time datum, unless otherwise stated in the UK AIP, is:

A Zulu

B UTC

C LMT

5 Aeronautical Information Circulars dealing with safety matters are:

A White

B Pink

C Green

6 You hear the following words on the radio from another aircraft:

"Pan Pan, Pan Pan, Pan Pan"

Which of the following statements is true?

A the aircraft is threatened by grave and imminent danger and requires immediate assistance.

B there is an urgency situation regarding the aircraft itself, or something or somebody in sight of the aircraft.

C the aircraft is threatened by grave and imminent danger but does not require immediate assistance.

7 The identification beacon at a civil aerodrome will show:

A A two letter morse group in green

B A two letter morse group in red

C An alternating white and green light

8 The identification beacon at a military aerodrome will show:

A A two letter morse group in green

B A two letter morse group in red

C An alternating white and green light

9 An aerodrome beacon will show:

A A two letter morse group in green

B A two letter morse group in red

C White flashing strobe light

10 In the UK AIP, unlicenced aerodromes are:

A Not listed in the AGA section

B Listed in the AGA section and these aerodromes have been inspected by the CAA

C Listed in the AGA section but the information has not been verified by the CAA

11 Aerodrome elevation given in the UK AIP AGA section is:

A The highest point on the manoeuvring area

B The highest point on the landing area

C The highest point on the aerodrome

12 PPR aerodromes may only be used when:

A Prior permission is obtained from the CAA

B Prior permission is obtained from NATS

C Prior permission is obtained from the owner

13 Emergency distance is defined as:

A The length of the runway plus stopway

B The length of the runway plus clearway

C The length of the runway only

14 If permission is given to operate into a military aerodrome liability for loss or damage is the responsibility of:

A The Ministry of Defence

B The CAA

C The aircraft operator

15 When VASIs are being used the aircraft is on the glidepath when:

A The near bars are red and the far bars are white

B The near bars are white and the far bars are red

C One of each of the pairs of lights of the near pair and the far pair is red and the other is white

---

16 If requesting a VDF bearing, a given bearing of Class Bravo is:

A accurate to within + or - 2°

B accurate to within + or - 5°

C accurate to within + or - 10°

---

17 When an AFIS service exists at an aerodrome, communications should not be attempted beyond:

A 5 nautical miles and 2000 feet

B 10 nautical miles and 3000 feet

C 25 nautical miles and 10 000 feet

---

18 The word INFORMATION in an aerodrome call-sign denotes:

A An aerodrome flight information service

B An aerodrome air/ground communication service

C An aerodrome tower service only

---

19 When a MAYDAY call is transmitted on 121.5 the message should be addressed to:

A West Drayton

B The ATIS in use

C No address is required

---

20 You pass your GFT on the 1st of February 1991 and your licence is issued on the 2nd June 1991. When is your Certificate of Experience due?

A 31st March 1992

B 1st July 1992

C 29th February 1992

1 When two aircraft are approaching head on:

A Each shall alter course to the right.

B Each shall alter course to the left.

C The smaller aircraft gives way by altering course to the right.

2 A captive balloon is required to show the appropriate lights at night providing it is more than:

A 60 meters above ground level.

B 60 feet above ground level.

C 100 meters above ground level.

3 A glider flying at night shall show the same lights as powered light aircraft or:

A A steady red light showing in all directions.

B A steady white light showing in all directions.

C A flashing red light showing in all directions.

4 When landings are not confined to a runway the commander of an aeroplane that is landing shall land to:

A The right of the aircraft ahead and clear to the left.

B Left of the aircraft ahead and clear to the right.

C Left of the aircraft ahead and clear to the left.

5 When several aircraft are making an approach to land, the one at the lowest altitude shall have the right of way unless:

A The lowest aircraft has cut in front of the other traffic.

B ATC has announced a different priority of landing.

C Any of the above apply.

6 VRP as shown on the 1:500 000 chart means:

A Verify radio position.

B Very high frequency radio range reporting point.

C Visual reporting point.

7 The navigation light on the starboard wing of an aircraft shall be:

A Red and visible through an arc of 110 degrees in the horizontal plane, from straight ahead to 20 degrees behind the wing, and visible through an arc of 180 degrees in the vertical plane.

B Green and visible through an arc of 110 degrees in the horizontal plane, from straight ahead to 20 degrees behind the wing, and visible through an arc of 180 degrees in the vertical plane.

C Green and visible through an arc of 140 degrees in the horizontal plane, 70 degrees either side of the centre line of the wing, visible through an arc of 180 degrees in the vertical plane.

8 An aircraft taxiing shall give way to;-

A All motor vehicles.

B A motor vehicle towing another aircraft.

C None of the above.

9 A flight plan may be filed;-

A Only when the pilot is required to do so by the AIC

B As (a) above or when the pilot is flying over sparsely populated areas

C For any flight

10 In order to comply with VFR outside controlled airspace, below 3000' amsl at an IAS of 130 kts, a fixed wing aircraft must:

A Remain 1000' horizontally from cloud

B Remain 1000' vertically from cloud

C Remain clear of cloud

11 In order to comply with licence privileges outside controlled airspace, below 3000' amsl at an IAS of 130 kts, a PPL without instrument qualification flying a fixed wing aircraft, with passengers, must:

A Have a flight visibility of at least 1500m

B Have a flight visibility of at least 5 KM

C Have a flight visibility of at least 3 KM

12 An aircraft flying under IFR outside controlled airspace would be permitted to fly at which of the following pressure altitudes:

A On a heading of 359°M, FL 310

B On a track of 359°M, FL 310

C On a track of 359°M, FL 290

13 A rectangular green flag flown from the mast of a UK aerodrome means:

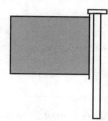

A That ATC is unmanned, but it is safe to proceed

B That right hand circuits are being flown

C That the runway to be used is at the discretion of the pilot

14 A white cross displayed at the end of a runway means that:

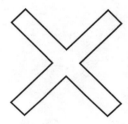

A The runway should be used in an emergency only

B The runway is not usable

C The runway may be used with caution

15 When flying outside controlled airspace, VFR, above 3000' AMSL, the altimeter sub-scale:

A must be set to 1013 mb/hpa.

B must be set to regional QNH.

C may be set to any desired setting.

16 When operating under a special VFR clearance the responsibility of remaining clear of ground obstructions rests with:

A The aircraft commander

B ATC

C Both of the above

17 When operating under a SVFR clearance:

A The aircraft commander must obey the 1500' rule at all times

B The aircraft commander may be required to disregard the 1500' rule

C The responsibility of keeping the aircraft clear of built up areas rests solely with ATC

18 As the owner/operator of a Cessna 152 (MAUW 757 KG) with an Aerial Work category C of A, what repairs may you carry out assuming you are not a licensed aircraft engineer:

A Any necessary for flight safety.

B Those prescribed in Regulation 16 of the Air Navigation (General) Regulations 1993.

C None

19 When flying outside controlled airspace below 3000' amsl the pilot may use:

A Any desired altimeter setting

B Only the regional QNH

C Either the regional QNH or the QNH of an adjacent aerodrome

20 A delay message should be initiated if a flight plan has been filed and the flight departure is delayed by:

A 30 minutes

B 1 hour

C 2 hours

1 A VFR full flight plan should be filed:

A 30 minutes before departure

B 60 minutes before clearance to start up or taxi is requested

C 60 minutes before the ETD

2 As a PPL you intend to make a private flight, carrying passengers, and share the cost between you. You may advertise this flight:

A Only in the local press.

B Only within a flying club if you will be flying one of that club's aeroplanes.

C Only within a flying club at the airfield where the flight will take place.

3 If, having filed a flight plan, the aircraft lands at an aerodrome other than the planned destination aerodrome:

A NATS will inform the planned destination aerodrome

B The pilot must inform the planned destination aerodrome within 30 minutes

C The pilot must inform the planned destination aerodrome within 30 minutes of his planned ETA at that aerodrome

4 Following what the pilot considers to be an airmiss situation the initial report should be made:

A By radio to the ATS unit being worked at the time

B By telephone to the CAA immediatly after landing

C By teleprinter using the AFTN immediately after landing

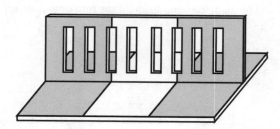

5 The above marker comprising a baseboard supporting a slatted vertical board, both striped orange/white/orange indicates :

A The boundary of a runway, taxiway or apron on grass airfield.

B The boundary of any part of a runway, taxiway or apron which is unfit for aircraft movment.

C The boundary of an aircraft parking area on a grass airfield

6 An aircraft has been intercepted and the intercepting aircraft makes an abrupt climbing turn through 90° or more, this means:

A Follow me

B You may proceed

C Turn around and fly on a reciprocal heading out of the restricted area you have entered, immediately

7 An aircraft which is intercepted by another should attempt to establish contact on the following frequency:

A The nearest MATZ

B 121.5 Mhz

C The FIR frequency

8 "Land after" procedure will only be used at civil aerodromes when the runway is long enough and:

A The second aircraft is able to keep the the first aircraft in sight at all times

B It is in daylight hours

C Both a and b above

9 A request for a MATZ penetration for civil aircraft should be made when:

A 15 nm or 5 minutes flying time from the MATZ boundary, whichever is the greater

B 15 nm or 5 minutes flying time from the aerodrome boundary, whichever is the greater

C At any time before penetrating the MATZ boundary

10 A "Finals" call should be made on completion of the turn onto final approach and at the range of:

A 10 nm

B 4 nm

C 10 km

11 A white letter L indicates a part of the manoeuvring area to be used:

A Only for aircraft less than 5700kg

B Only for aircraft less than 2300kg

C Only for the taking off and landing of light aircraft

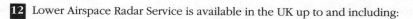

12 Lower Airspace Radar Service is available in the UK up to and including:

A The transition altitude

✓ B FL 95

C FL 245

13 If an aircraft has inadvertently entered or is about to enter a restricted, prohibited or danger area, the pilot may receive a warning in the form of:

A Alternating red and green lights or flares

B Black and white smoke shells by day and white star shells by night

✓ C Projectiles which on bursting show red and green lights

14 The UK military low flying system extends from the surface to;-

A 500 feet AGL

B 1000 feet AGL

✓ C 2000 feet AGL

15 In the event of a forced landing in the UK after flying inbound from a non EC airport, passengers and cargo may be removed from the aircraft:

A At the discretion of the commander

✓ B With the permission of a customs and excise officer or in an emergency

C Only in an emergency

16 Immediately before a flight in the UK, you want to check if the Queen is going flying too. You can check this:

A By telephoning Buckingham Palace.

✓ B On a specially provided Freephone number, available to all.

C Only from R NOTAMS, distributed by post.

17 You are a PPL without any instrument qualification. You are flying a Cessna 172 (IAS 105 Knots), with a passenger, outside controlled airspace at 2500 feet QNH. What is the minimum flight visibility (i) for you to legally operate in (ii) for VFR flight

A (i) 3KM   (ii) any 'reasonable' visibility

✓ B (i) 5 KM   (ii) 1500m

C (i) 5 KM   (ii) 5 KM

18 A continuous red light directed at an aircraft in flight, from ATC, means:

A Do not land, wait for permission.

B Do not land, aerodrome not available for landing.

✓ C Give way to other aircraft and continue circling.

19 An aircraft involved in SAR seen rocking its wings is:

A Likely to be in turbulent air

B Directing a surface craft towards an aircraft or surface craft in distress

C Directing another aircraft towards an aircraft or surface craft in distress

20 A ground air visual signal in the shape of the letter V means:

A Assistance is required

B Medical assistance is required

C Proceed in the direction indicated by the point of the V

1 It is mandatory to keep a technical log in respect of:

A   All UK registered aircraft only when flying for the purpose of public transport.

B   All UK registered aircraft with a C of A either in the transport or aerial work category for all flights.

C   All UK registered aircraft with a C of A in the transport or aerial work category only when carrying passengers.

2 As a holder of a UK flying licence you must inform the CAA of any illness which prevents you undertaking the duties to which the licence relates after a period of:

A   21 days

B   14 days

C   7 days

3 Personal flying logbook entries shall be completed in respect of each and every flight:

A   As soon as is reasonably practical

B   Within 24 hours of completion of the flight

C   By midnight the day after the flight ended

4 A person acting as a member of the crew of any aircraft shall not be permitted to do so if:

A   He/she has consumed any alcohol within the past 8 hours

B   He/she has consumed any alcohol within the past 5 hours

C   If the consumption of alcohol or drugs has impaired his/her ability so to act

5 If requested to do so by an authorised person, the commander of an aircraft must produce the certificate of registration of the aircraft and his pilots licence within:

A   5 days

B   15 days

C   a reasonable time

6 For the purpose of exercising PPL privileges without a night rating, night is defined as:

A   Dusk to dawn

B   Sunset to sunrise

C   30 minutes after sunset to 30 minutes before sunrise

7 For the purpose of the ANO an aircraft is deemed to be in flight:

A   From the moment the wheels leave the ground to the moment they touch down again

B   From the moment the aircraft moves under its own power, with the intent to fly, to the moment it comes to rest after landing

C   As in 'a' above plus 10 minutes for taxying

8 Orange/white wedge shaped markers (like elongated wheel chocks in shape) alternating with square flags showing equal orange and white triangular areas, as shown below, indicate:

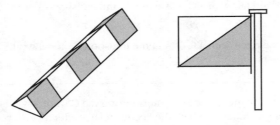

A The boundary of an aircraft parking area on a grass airfield.

B The boundary of a runway, taxiway or apron on a grass airfield.

C The boundary of any part of a runway, taxiway or apron which is unfit for aircraft movment.

9 A powered aircraft may not fly over a congested area below the following defined limits:

A 1500 feet above the highest fixed obstacle within 2000 feet of the aircraft

B 1500 feet above the highest fixed obstacle within 2000 metres of the aircraft

C 1500 feet above the highest fixed obstacle within 5 nm of the aircraft

10 An aircraft may not fly over a gathering of 1000 or more people who are witnessing or participating in any organised event within:

A 1500 feet

B 2000 feet

C 3000 feet

11 When simulated instrument flying is being undertaken and the view of the safety pilot is restricted it is necessary to carry a third person who can see the areas in the safety pilot's blind spots, and who can communicate with him. This third person must be:

A A competent observer

B A PPL holder

C At least a student pilot

12 The correct quadrantal for a aircraft flying on a magnetic track of 180° is:

A FL 180

B FL190

C FL195

13 A white dumbell with black stripes across each disc at right angles to the shaft indicates:

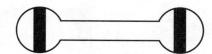

A All movements are confined to paved areas

B Take-off and landing is confined to the paved areas but aircraft may taxi on the grass

C Aircraft may take-off and land on the grass if they wish

14 A red square with a yellow diagonal inside the the signal square indicates:

A Landing is prohibited

B The state of the manoeuvring area is poor

C Aircraft may only land on paved areas

15 A continuous red light directed at an aircraft on the ground means:

A The aircraft must stop

B The aircraft must return to the parking bay

C The aircraft may continue to the hold but must not take-off

16 A marshaller with arms extended, palms facing inwards, then swung from the extended position inwards, indicates:

A The chocks are inserted

B The chocks have been removed

C Insert control locks

17 A succession of white pyrotechnic lights fired from an aircraft in flight indicates:

A It is in imminent danger and requires immediate assistance

B It is compelled to land

C It has suffered a total communication failure

18 You make a private flight with two passengers. The flight lasts for 1 hour 30 minutes at a cost of £60 per hour. Under the cost-sharing provisions what is the pilot's minimum contribution to the costs?

A £25.00

B £20.00

C £30.00

19 You are flying at night and observe the green navigation light of another aircraft on a constant relative bearing of 330°:

A There is no risk of collision

B There is a risk of collision , you have the right of way, but be prepared to alter course if the other aircraft fails to give way

C There is risk of collision, alter course to the left to pass behind the other aircraft

20 A free balloon whilst flying at night shall display:

A A steady red light between 5 and 10 metres below the balloon or basket

B A steady white light between 5 and 10 metres below the balloon or basket

C A steady red light between 4 and 8 metres below the balloon or basket and a steady white light 4 metres below the red light

1 A pilot of a microlight (Group D) aircraft, not under instruction, must hold a Pilot's licence:

A For all flights

B Only if the microlight is registered with the CAA

C Only when carrying passengers

2 Which of the following Flight Levels would be appropriate for flight under IFR outside controlled airspace on a track of 005° (T), variation 11° E (below FL 245):

A 55

B 60

C 65

3 An aircraft with a valid Certificate of Airworthiness also has a weight schedule produced. This weight schedule must be kept for:

A Six months after a subsequent weighing

B Thirteen months after a subsequent weighing

C Until any subsequent weighing

4 A rectangular red/yellow chequered flag or board means;:

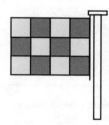

A Aircraft may move on the manoeuvring area and apron only with permission of ATC.

B Aircraft may move on the manoeuvring area only with the permission of ATC.

C Aircraft may move on the apron only with the permission of ATC.

5 The UK Wake Vortex spacing minima for a light aircraft taking off behind a heavy aircraft from the same point is:

A 2 mins

B 3 mins

C 4 mins

6 In flight by night you see only the red navigation light of another aircraft flying at approximately the same level as your aircraft, and on a constant relative bearing of 060°:

A Alter course to port

B Alter course to starboard

C Maintain heading and speed but be prepared to take action

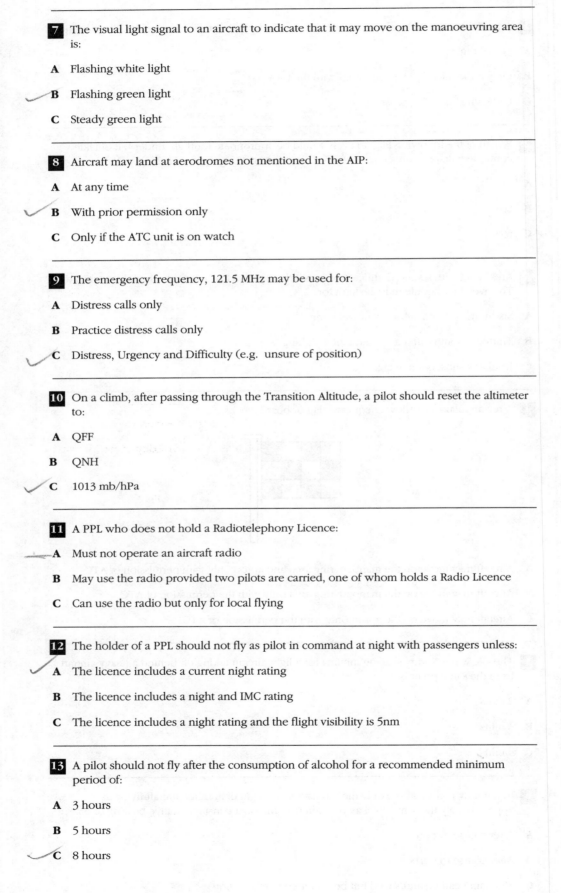

7 The visual light signal to an aircraft to indicate that it may move on the manoeuvring area is:

A Flashing white light

B Flashing green light

C Steady green light

8 Aircraft may land at aerodromes not mentioned in the AIP:

A At any time

B With prior permission only

C Only if the ATC unit is on watch

9 The emergency frequency, 121.5 MHz may be used for:

A Distress calls only

B Practice distress calls only

C Distress, Urgency and Difficulty (e.g. unsure of position)

10 On a climb, after passing through the Transition Altitude, a pilot should reset the altimeter to:

A QFF

B QNH

C 1013 mb/hPa

11 A PPL who does not hold a Radiotelephony Licence:

A Must not operate an aircraft radio

B May use the radio provided two pilots are carried, one of whom holds a Radio Licence

C Can use the radio but only for local flying

12 The holder of a PPL should not fly as pilot in command at night with passengers unless:

A The licence includes a current night rating

B The licence includes a night and IMC rating

C The licence includes a night rating and the flight visibility is 5nm

13 A pilot should not fly after the consumption of alcohol for a recommended minimum period of:

A 3 hours

B 5 hours

C 8 hours

14 A rectangular red flag on a signal mast at an aerodrome means:

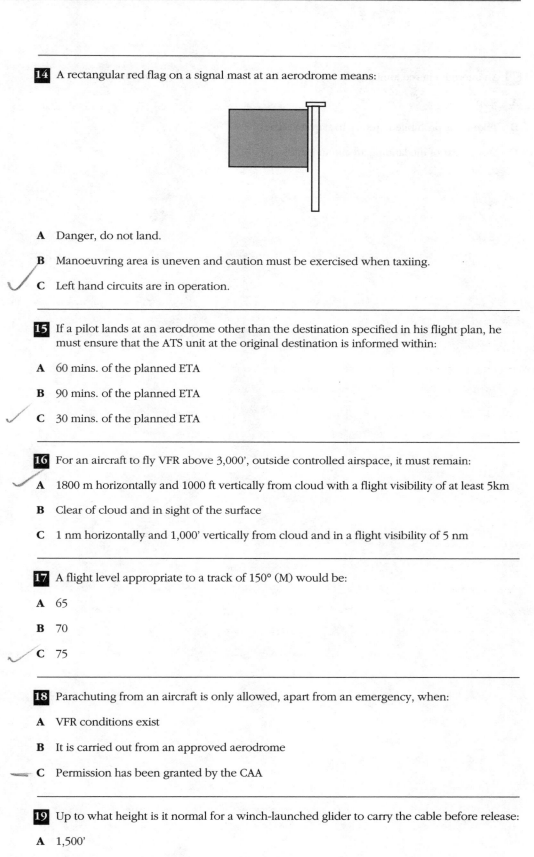

A Danger, do not land.

B Manoeuvring area is uneven and caution must be exercised when taxiing.

C Left hand circuits are in operation.

15 If a pilot lands at an aerodrome other than the destination specified in his flight plan, he must ensure that the ATS unit at the original destination is informed within:

A 60 mins. of the planned ETA

B 90 mins. of the planned ETA

C 30 mins. of the planned ETA

16 For an aircraft to fly VFR above 3,000', outside controlled airspace, it must remain:

A 1800 m horizontally and 1000 ft vertically from cloud with a flight visibility of at least 5km

B Clear of cloud and in sight of the surface

C 1 nm horizontally and 1,000' vertically from cloud and in a flight visibility of 5 nm

17 A flight level appropriate to a track of 150° (M) would be:

A 65

B 70

C 75

18 Parachuting from an aircraft is only allowed, apart from an emergency, when:

A VFR conditions exist

B It is carried out from an approved aerodrome

C Permission has been granted by the CAA

19 Up to what height is it normal for a winch-launched glider to carry the cable before release:

A 1,500'

B 2,000'

C 2,500'

20 An intermittent red luminous beam directed at an aircraft on the ground means:

A Stop

B Take-off is prohibited...return to starting place

C Move clear of the landing area immediately

1 The following Flight Level complies with the quadrantal rules for a magnetic track of 270°:

A   95

B   105

C   110

2 Outside controlled airspace and below 3,000' amsl and subject to certain exceptions, the only rule for IFR Flight is that:

A   An aircraft in level flight shall be flown in accordance with the quadrantal flight rule

B   The aircraft must be flown at a height of not less than 1,000' above the highest fixed object within 5nm of the aircraft

C   The aircraft must remain clear of cloud and in sight of the surface

3 A marshaller holding his right or left arm down and the other arm moved across the body and extended means:

A   Turn in the direction indicated by the extended arm.

B   Proceed under guidance of another marshaller who's position is indicated by the extended arm.

C   Open up engine indicated by extended arm.

4 A PPL whose licence does not include an Instrument Rating or an IMC Rating, flying outside controlled airspace, must comply with a minimum visibility of:

A   5 km if carrying passengers, 3 km if solo

B   3 nm if carrying passengers, 1 nm if solo

C   8 km if carrying passengers, 5 km if solo

5 When two flying machines at approximately the same altitude are converging, what initial action should be taken by the aircraft which has the other on it's left?

A   Maintain heading and speed

B   Climb or descend to a different level

C   Give way to the other aircraft, but avoid passing over, under, or in front of it

6 An aircraft following a landmark such as a railway line, should keep the feature:

A   On its left

B   On its right

C   Either

7 You are taxying out from an apron, when you see an aircraft being towed, converging with you from your left-hand side. Who has right-of-way?

A   You

B   The aircraft being towed

C   Both have equal claim to right-of-way

8 A marshaller starting with arms extended, palms facing inwards, then swinging the arms inwards from the extended position indicates:

A Chocks inserted.

B Reduce the hover height (Helicopters) and prepare to touch down.

C Chocks away.

9 If a PPL is ill and his illness renders him incapable of acting as pilot, it must be notified to the CAA:

A As soon as possible

B After 20 days of illness have elapsed

C Only if a Medical Examiner advises

10 Rules of the Air apply to all UK- registered aircraft:

A Wherever they fly

B Only in the UK

C Only in controlled airspace

11 A white dumbbell in the signals area means:

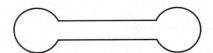

A Movement of aircraft is confined to paved or hard surfaces

B Movement of aircraft for take-off and landing is confined to paved or hard surfaces, but taxying is permitted on the grass

C Aerodrome closed for all movements

12 An aircraft shall not fly over any congested area below a height that would permit it to alight clear in the event of an engine failure, without danger to the property or persons, or below a specified height. This height is:

A Not less than 1,000' above the highest fixed object within 1,500'

B Not less than 1,000' above the highest fixed object within 2,000'

C Not less than 1,500' above the highest fixed object within 2,000'

13 A continuous red light directed to an aircraft on the ground means:

A Proceed to the holding point, and await further clearance

B Stop

C Stop until conflicting traffic has passed

14 The characteristics of identification beacons at civil aerodromes are:

A A two letter morse group in green

B A three letter morse group in green

C A two letter morse group in red

15 A pilot has filed a full flight plan to a UK aerodrome that does not have an ATSU. Which of the following statements is most correct?

A The pilot can always close the flight plan on arrival by telephoning the departure aerodrome.

B The pilot can nominate anybody as a responsible person.

C If the parent ATSU hears nothing, they assume the flight has arrived safely.

16 A square yellow board bearing a black C indicates:

A The aerodrome canteen.

B Customs.

C The place at which a pilot can report to ATC or other aerodrome authority.

17 An aircraft must not be flown closer to any person, vessel or structure than:

A 700'

B 1,000'

C 500'

18 When flying on a northerly heading, you see the green navigation light and anti-collision light of another flying machine on a relative bearing of 045° distance about 5nm. If both aircraft continue on course:

A There may be a risk of collision and you should alter heading

B There may be a risk of collision but you have the right of way

C There is no risk of collision

19 In order for an altimeter to read altitude, the sub-scale should be set to:

A QFE

B QNH

C 1013 mb (Hp)

20 The colour marking for ground refuelling equipment and fuel filler points for Avgas is:

A Black

B Green

C Red

1 White flashes directed from ATC to an aircraft in flight means:

A Follow the directions being given in morse code by the flashing lights.

B Land at this aerodrome after receiving continuous green light.

C Return to your starting point.

2 A yellow cross indicates:

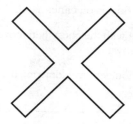

A The section of the runway or taxiway so marked is un-fit for the movment of aircraft.

B Tow ropes and similar articles may be dropped only in the area in which the cross is placed.

C The airfield may only be used for landings in an emergency.

3 A marshaller repeatedly crossing his arms above his head is indicating:

A Move forward.

B Move back.

C Stop.

4 With certain exceptions an aircraft may not normally fly closer than 500' to:

A The surface.

B Another aircraft.

C A person, vessel, vehicle or structure.

5 By day, your aircraft is intercepted by an interceptor aircraft that takes up position ahead and to the left of you and rocks its wings. The meaning of this signal, and your acknowledgement to comply is:

A Follow me. Your aircraft lowers undercarrage.

B You may proceed. Your aircraft rocks wings.

C Follow me. Your aircraft rocks wings.

6 An aircraft is following a surface line feature (such as a motorway). To comply with the rules of the air:

A The aircraft should be to the left of the line feature.

B The line feature should be to the left of the aircraft.

C The line feature should be to the right of the aircraft.

7 Outside controlled airspace, a transponder is required for flight:

A At and above FL100.

B In a MATZ.

C When using a RAS or RIS service.

8 A marshaller indicating to a pilot to cut engines will:

A Make a scissor action with two fingers on either hand.

B Place either arm and hand level with the chest then move the hand laterally across the chest with the palm facing downwards.

C Place either arm and hand at shoulder level, drawing the hand across the throat (as if cutting).

9 In relation to minor repairs and replacements, the owner or operator of an aircraft who is not a licenced engineer, but who holds a pilots licence:

A Can do no work under any circumstances.

B May do certain work subject to the provisions of the Air Navigation (General) Regulations.

C Can do any work so long as the aircraft has a special category Certificate Of Airworthiness.

10 In relation to the '1500 feet' and 'glide clear' requirements of the low flying rules for flight over a congested area, exemption is given to:

A Helicopters.

B Aircraft carrying out forced landing training.

C CAA aircraft.

11 Standard aerodrome signals are displayed:

A Close to the runway in use.

B As close as possible to the centre of the aerodrome.

C In a signals area close to the ATS unit.

12 In relation to allowing or causing an aircraft to endanger persons or property, the law applies to:

A Flying Instructors only.

B Any pilot.

C Any person.

13 An aircraft in flight, signalling to an aerodrome that it is compelled to land does so using:

A A continuous green, or green flashes, or a green pyrotechnic light.

B White pyrotechnic lights or switching on and off the navigation lights, or switching on and off the landing lights or white flashes.

C Red pyrotechnic light, or red flare.

14 An interceptor aircraft, wishing to signal that the intercepted aircraft should proceed will:

A Switch navigation lights on and off at irregular intervals.

B Make an abrupt climbing turn through at least 90°.

C Rock its wings and make a slow left turn.

15 An Air Traffic Controller can close a licenced aerodrome:

A When the landing area is unfit.

B For weather reasons.

C When there is nobody available to collect landing fees.

16 Responsibility for checking aircraft loading before a flight rests with:

A The aircraft commander.

B The aircraft operator, or person designated by the operator.

C The aircraft manufacturer.

17 A white disc at the head of a white T in the signal area means:

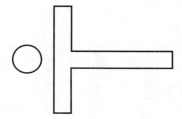

A The direction of landing and the direction of taking off do not necessarily coincide.

B The direction of landing and the direction of taking off are the same.

C Caution, parachute drop zone close to direction of take off and landing.

18 A red and yellow striped arrow bent through 90 degrees around the edge of the signals area and pointing in a clockwise direction means:

A A right handed circuit is in operation.

B Vacate the runway to the right immediately after landing.

C Follow the arrows to the check in point after parking your aircraft.

19 When using PAPIs, the pilot of a light aircraft is on the correct approach slope when:

A Two red and two green lights are visible.

B The two outer lights are red, the two inner lights are white.

C The two lights nearest the runway are red, the two lights furthest from the runway white.

20 The correct transponder code to indicate an emergency situation is:

A 7000

B 7700

C 4321

Instructions

1 Time allowed 60 minutes.

2 Twenty multi choice questions each carrying 5 marks. Marks are not deducted for wrong answers. The pass mark is 70%.

3 Read each question carefully as there is only one answer which is correct.

4 Remember examination technique, you are advised to pass over questions that seem difficult at first sight and return to them when you have answered the others.

1 If you were flying into an area of low pressure, what drift, if any, would you experience in the Northern Hemisphere?

A Starboard

B None

C Port

2 The observed temperature at the surface is +11°C and at 4,000ft it is +16°C. The state of the atmosphere can be described as:

A Moist

B Unstable

C Stable

3 Which of the following conditions is most favourable for the formation of carburettor icing if the aircraft is descending with glide power?

	Relative Humidity	Ambient temp
A	25%	+25°C
B	40%	+30°C
C	50%	-10°C

4 At an inland airfield in Central Southern England at 2300 hours which of the following sets of conditions is most likely to lead to the formation of radiation fog?

	w/v	Cloud Cover	Temperature	Dew Point
A	10 kts	5/8 st	+12	+11
B	10 kts	NIL	+15	+12
C	3 kts	1/8 ci	+8	+7

5 Steady Precipitation in contrast to showers, preceding a front is related to;-

A Stratiform cloud with moderate turbulence

B Cumuloform cloud with little or no turbulence

C Shallow stratiform clouds with little or no turbulence

REFER TO APPENDIX 1
Appendix shows a typical warm sector depression (polar front)
Draw in the expected cloud types and precipitation.

6 What cloud type would you expect in I 6 and what visibility and precipitation?

A Cumulus, Good Visibility, Showers

B Stratus, Poor Visibility, Drizzle

C Stratocumulus, Good Visibility, Heavy Showers

7 What cloud would you expect in L 2?

A Ci

B Cu

C As

8 In the UK, away from exposed coasts, airmass thunderstorms are most likely in:

A Warm spells in winter

B The evenings with westerly winds in summer

C The afternoon in summer

9 As a warm front passes the weather is:

A Slight showers, moderate continuous drizzle

B Moderate continuous rain, intermittent slight drizzle

C Moderate continuous rain, rain showers

10 The cloud sequence associated with the passage of a cold front is?

A Cu/Cb Ns + low St:

B St Cu/Cb + BKN St or prob 30 low NS

C Cu/Cb Isol Cu

11 Cloud bases in TAFs, Metars & synoptic charts are given in:

A Heights above mean sea level

B Heights above 1013.2 mb pressure level

C Heights above official airfield level

12 Which of the following processes can produce both fog and cloud?

A Divergence

B Advection

C Convection

13 The wind which results from air cooling on the side of a valley is known as:

A A katabatic wind

B A valley wind

C An anabatic wind

14 Which of the conditions given below is most likely to lead to the formation of radiation fog?

	Wind speed	Cloud cover	Temperature	Dewpoint
A	7 kt	8/8 st	12°C	11°C
B	15 kt	NIL	15°C	14°C
C	3 kt	1/8 ci	8°C	7°C

15 In which of the following situations is carburettor icing most likely to be serious over NW Europe?

A Summer, warm, Descent power

B Summer, warm, Cruise power

C Winter, cold, Descent power

16 The lowest layer of the atmosphere is:

A The Stratosphere

B The Troposphere

C The Mesosphere

REFER TO LAPFORM ONE

17 What is the 2000' wind at EBBR?

A 170/25

B 120/25

C 145/30

18 What is the surface temperature at 55N 05E (assume no cloud)?

A +18°C

B +12°F

C +17°C

19 What time UTC will the cold front reach the Isle of Wight - i.e. front has to travel 40nm?

A 17:00

B 17:40

C 19:00

20 What are the worst conditions of turbulence in zone 2?

A Light

B Severe

C Moderate

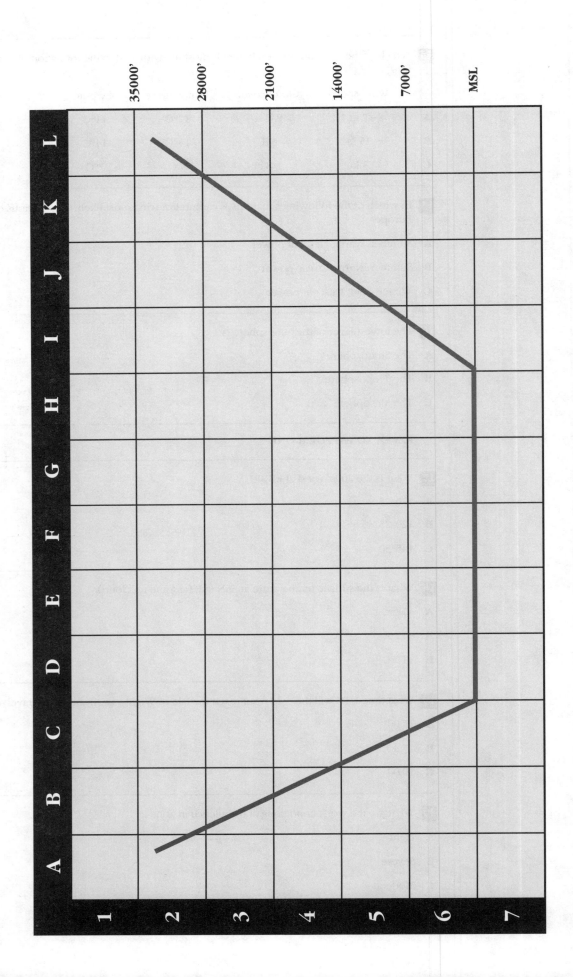

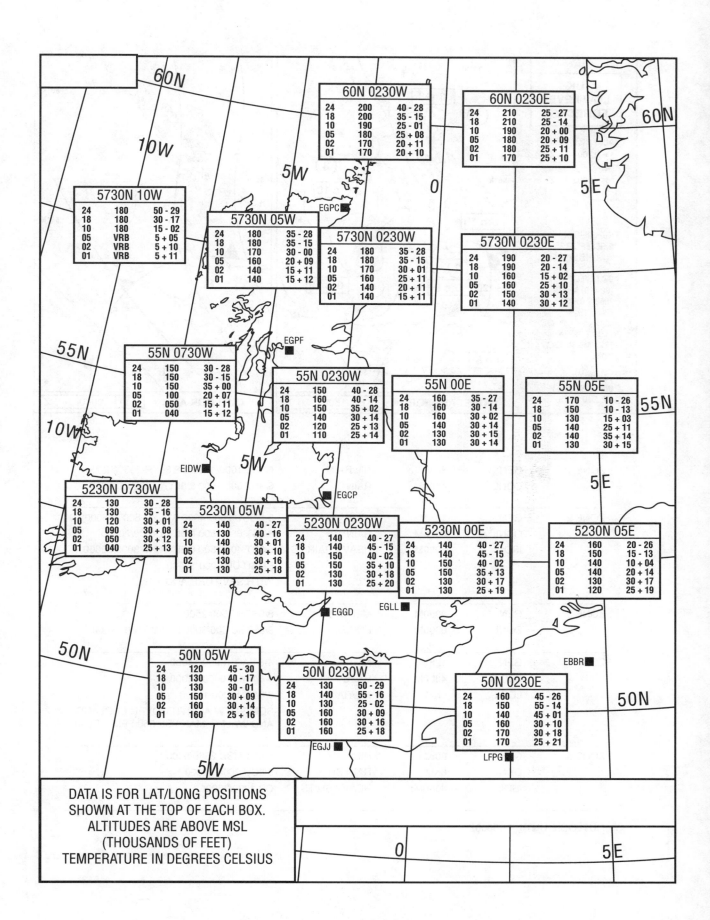

60N 0230W

24	200	40 - 28
18	200	35 - 15
10	190	25 - 01
05	180	25 + 08
02	170	20 + 11
01	170	20 + 10

60N 0230E

24	210	25 - 27
18	210	25 - 14
10	190	20 + 00
05	180	20 + 09
02	180	25 + 11
01	170	25 + 10

5730N 10W

24	180	50 - 29
18	180	30 - 17
10	180	15 - 02
05	VRB	5 + 05
02	VRB	5 + 10
01	VRB	5 + 11

5730N 05W

24	180	35 - 28
18	180	35 - 15
10	170	30 - 00
05	160	20 + 09
02	140	15 + 11
01	140	15 + 12

5730N 0230W

24	180	35 - 28
18	180	35 - 15
10	170	30 + 01
05	160	25 + 11
02	140	20 + 11
01	140	15 + 11

5730N 0230E

24	190	20 - 27
18	190	20 - 14
10	160	15 + 02
05	160	25 + 10
02	150	30 + 13
01	140	30 + 12

55N 0730W

24	150	30 - 28
18	150	30 - 15
10	150	35 + 00
05	100	20 + 07
02	050	15 + 11
01	040	15 + 12

55N 0230W

24	150	40 - 28
18	160	40 - 14
10	150	35 + 02
05	140	30 + 14
02	120	25 + 13
01	110	25 + 14

55N 00E

24	160	35 - 27
18	160	30 - 14
10	160	30 + 02
05	140	30 + 14
02	130	30 + 15
01	130	30 + 14

55N 05E

24	170	10 - 26
18	150	10 - 13
10	130	15 + 03
05	140	25 + 11
02	140	35 + 14
01	130	30 + 15

5230N 0730W

24	130	30 - 28
18	130	35 - 16
10	120	30 + 01
05	090	30 + 08
02	050	30 + 12
01	040	25 + 13

5230N 05W

24	140	40 - 27
18	130	40 - 16
10	140	30 + 01
05	140	30 + 10
02	130	30 + 16
01	130	25 + 18

5230N 0230W

24	140	40 - 27
18	140	45 - 15
10	150	40 - 02
05	150	35 + 10
02	130	30 + 18
01	130	25 + 20

5230N 00E

24	140	40 - 27
18	140	45 - 15
10	150	40 - 02
05	150	35 + 13
02	130	30 + 17
01	130	25 + 19

5230N 05E

24	160	20 - 26
18	150	15 - 13
10	140	10 + 04
05	140	20 + 14
02	130	30 + 17
01	120	25 + 19

50N 05W

24	120	45 - 30
18	130	40 - 17
10	130	30 - 01
05	150	30 + 09
02	160	30 + 14
01	160	25 + 16

50N 0230W

24	130	50 - 29
18	140	55 - 16
10	130	25 - 02
05	160	30 + 09
02	160	30 + 16
01	160	25 + 18

50N 0230E

24	160	45 - 26
18	150	55 - 14
10	140	45 + 01
05	160	30 + 10
02	170	30 + 18
01	170	25 + 21

Station markers: EGPC, EGPF, EIDW, EGCP, EGGD, EGLL, EBBR, EGJJ, LFPG

DATA IS FOR LAT/LONG POSITIONS
SHOWN AT THE TOP OF EACH BOX.
ALTITUDES ARE ABOVE MSL
(THOUSANDS OF FEET)
TEMPERATURE IN DEGREES CELSIUS

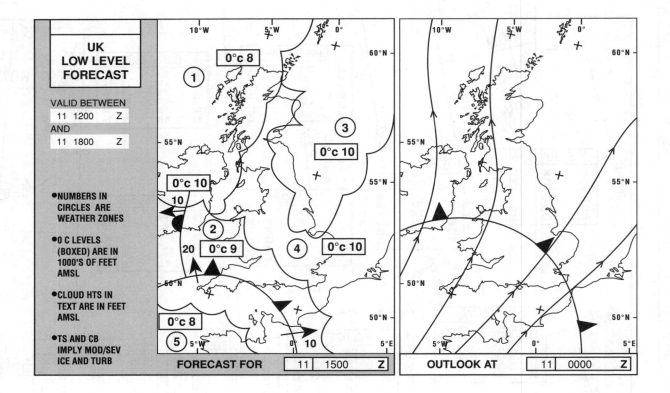

| | | UK LOW LEVEL FORECAST | VALID BETWEEN 11 1200 Z AND 11 1800 Z | | FORECAST FOR 11 1500 Z | | OUTLOOK AT 11 0000 Z |

- NUMBERS IN CIRCLES ARE WEATHER ZONES
- 0 C LEVELS (BOXED) ARE IN 1000'S OF FEET AMSL
- CLOUD HTS IN TEXT ARE IN FEET AMSL
- TS AND CB IMPLY MOD/SEV ICE AND TURB

ZONE 1	GEN	8KM	NIL/RAIN	6/8ST 1000/1500 6-8/8LYR 2500/12000
	OCNL	4000M	RAIN	6/8ST 500/1500 8/8LYR 15000/19000
ZONE 2	GEN	10KM	NIL/RAIN	3-5/8SC 2000/4000 6/8LYR 8000/16000
	OCNL	4000M	RAIN	6/8ST 600/1500 8/8LYR 4000/20000
	ISOL	2000M	HEAVY RAIN/TS	5/8ST 400/1500 8/8LYR NS 3000/20000 + EMBD CB 5000/36000 WITH SEV TURB AND ICE.
ZONE 3	GEN	3000M	MIST/DZ	8/8STSC 500/2500
	OCNL	0300M	FOG/DZ	8/8STSC 000/3000 3/8AC 7000/14000
ZONE 4	GEN	12KM	NIL	4-6/8AC 10000/14000
	LOC N	4000M	HAZE	4-6/8AC 10000/14000
	LOC S	8KM	NIL/RAIN	6/8AC 10000/16000 SOME MTW ACTIVITY OVER ENGLAND AND WALES. MAX VSP 350 FPM AT 090.
ZONE 5	GEN	30KM	NIL	4-6/8CUSC 2500/5000
	OCNL	6KM	RAIN SH	5/8CU 2000/12000
	ISOL	4000M	HEAVY SH/TS	CB 1000/30000

OUTLOOK: UNTIL 11/0000Z:

1 You are flying to an airfield on the east coast. You suspect a sea breeze will be blowing when you arrive, what is the most likely direction of the surface wind?

A 350 degrees

B 100 degrees

C 260 degrees

2 The rate of fall of pressure with height is:

A Greater in cold air than warm

B Greater in warm air than cold

C Inversely proportional to temp

3 The average change of pressure with height in the lower layers of the atmosphere is:

A 1mb/30ft

B 1mb/20ft

C 1mb/50ft

4 A body of air over the ocean is referred to as:

A Polar air

B Oceanic air

C Maritime air

5 Over which of the following, do you expect the greatest diurnal range of temperature to occur:

A An extensive forest area

B A desert area

C An ocean

6 You are planning a flight to an airfield where wind shear has been reported. Which of the following describes the appropriate pre-flight action?

A Check the aircraft's insurance

B Reduce fuel load so that you can approach slower

C Check fuel load and alternates with a view to holding/diverting if necessary

7 An inversion means that the temperature.......... as height increases

A Increases

B Decreases

C Remains constant

8 A line on a chart joining places of equal sea level pressure is called an:

A Isogonal

B Agonic line

C Isobar

9 An aircraft, flying so that the altimeter indicates 2500ft with the current regional QNH set in the subscale, is flying towards an area of lower pressure. If the pilot fails to revise the sub-scale setting as the QNH changes, then the aircraft will:

A Gradually climb

B Gradually descend

C Maintain 2500ft AMSL

10 The temperature at sea level in the ISA is:

A +12.5°C

B +25°C

C +15°C

11 A wind whose direction has changed clockwise in direction has:

A Reduced

B Backed

C Veered

12 The wind that flows around curved isobars is called the:

A Gradient Wind

B Geostrophic Wind

C Isobaric Wind

13 If the wind at altitude is 240/35, the most likely wind on the ground is:

A 270/40

B 220/20

C 220/40

14 "LUMPY" or "HEAPED" cloud can be classified as:

A Stratus

B Cumulus

C Cirrus

15 As a parcel of air cools, its ability to hold water vapour:

A Decreases

B Increases

C Remains unaltered

16 The three stages of a thunderstorm's life are:

A Building, Dissipating, Mature

B Mature, Building, Dissipating

C Building, Mature, Dissipating

REFER TO LAPFORM 2

17 The abbreviation BKN means

A   1-4 oktas cloud cover

B   3-7 oktas cloud cover

C   5-7 oktas cloud cover

18 In the warnings for zone 4 the following is indicated:

A   Mountain wave activity, maximum vertical speed 350 at 900'

B   Mountain wave activity, maximum vertical speed 350 feet per minute at 9000'

C   Mountain wave activity, vertical speed exceeding 350 fpm at FL90.

19 The 2000' wind at EGLL is

A   130/25

B   130/30

C   145/30

20 In zone 5, the cloud includes

A   5 oktas of cumulus between 20000 and 12000 feet

B   Cumulonimbus between 10000 and 30000 feet

C   4-6 oktas of cumulus and stratocumulus between 2500 and 5000 feet.

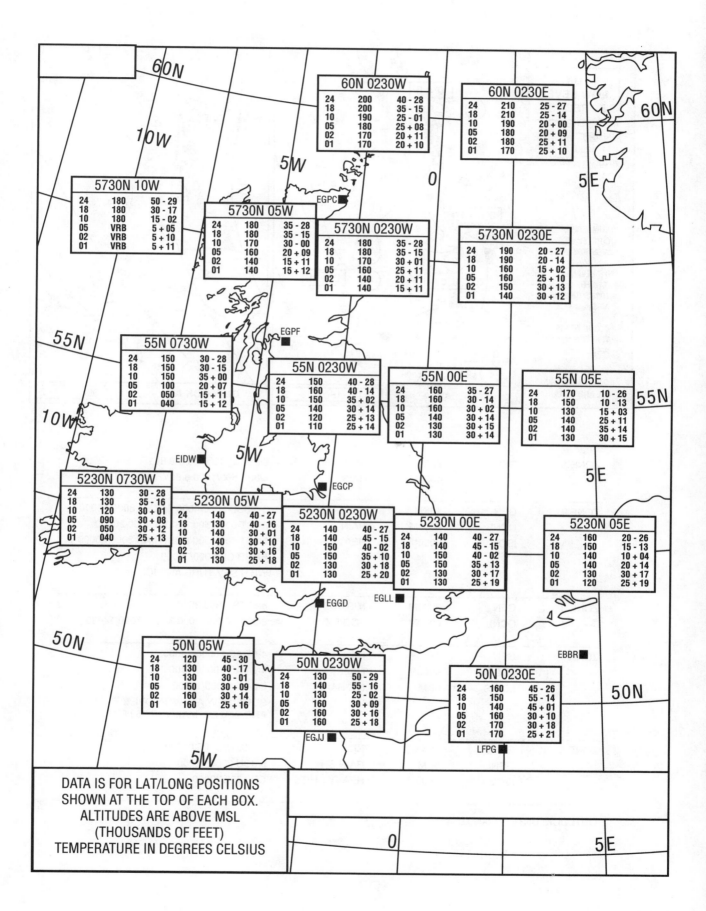

60N 0230W

24	200	40 - 28
18	200	35 - 15
10	190	25 - 01
05	180	25 + 08
02	170	20 + 11
01	170	20 + 10

60N 0230E

24	210	25 - 27
18	210	25 - 14
10	190	20 + 00
05	180	20 + 09
02	180	25 + 11
01	170	25 + 10

5730N 10W

24	180	50 - 29
18	180	30 - 17
10	180	15 - 02
05	VRB	5 + 05
02	VRB	5 + 10
01	VRB	5 + 11

5730N 05W

24	180	35 - 28
18	180	35 - 15
10	170	30 - 00
05	160	20 + 09
02	140	15 + 11
01	140	15 + 12

5730N 0230W

24	180	35 - 28
18	180	35 - 15
10	170	30 + 01
05	160	25 + 11
02	140	20 + 11
01	140	15 + 11

5730N 0230E

24	190	20 - 27
18	190	20 - 14
10	160	15 + 02
05	160	25 + 10
02	150	30 + 13
01	140	30 + 12

55N 0730W

24	150	30 - 28
18	150	30 - 15
10	150	35 + 00
05	100	20 + 07
02	050	15 + 11
01	040	15 + 12

55N 0230W

24	150	40 - 28
18	160	40 - 14
10	150	35 + 02
05	140	30 + 14
02	120	25 + 13
01	110	25 + 14

55N 00E

24	160	35 - 27
18	160	30 - 14
10	160	30 + 02
05	140	30 + 14
02	130	30 + 15
01	130	30 + 14

55N 05E

24	170	10 - 26
18	150	10 - 13
10	130	15 + 03
05	140	25 + 11
02	140	35 + 14
01	130	30 + 15

5230N 0730W

24	130	30 - 28
18	130	35 - 16
10	120	30 + 01
05	090	30 + 08
02	050	30 + 12
01	040	25 + 13

5230N 05W

24	140	40 - 27
18	130	40 - 16
10	140	30 + 01
05	140	30 + 10
02	130	30 + 14
01	130	25 + 18

5230N 0230W

24	140	40 - 27
18	140	45 - 15
10	150	40 - 02
05	150	35 + 10
02	130	30 + 18
01	130	25 + 20

5230N 00E

24	140	40 - 27
18	140	45 - 15
10	150	40 - 02
05	150	35 + 13
02	130	30 + 17
01	130	25 + 19

5230N 05E

24	160	20 - 26
18	150	15 - 13
10	140	10 + 04
05	140	20 + 14
02	130	30 + 17
01	120	25 + 19

50N 05W

24	120	45 - 30
18	130	40 - 17
10	130	30 - 01
05	150	30 + 09
02	160	30 + 14
01	160	25 + 16

50N 0230W

24	130	50 - 29
18	140	55 - 16
10	130	25 - 02
05	160	30 + 09
02	160	30 + 16
01	160	25 + 18

50N 0230E

24	160	45 - 26
18	150	55 - 14
10	140	45 + 01
05	160	30 + 10
02	170	30 + 18
01	170	25 + 21

DATA IS FOR LAT/LONG POSITIONS
SHOWN AT THE TOP OF EACH BOX.
ALTITUDES ARE ABOVE MSL
(THOUSANDS OF FEET)
TEMPERATURE IN DEGREES CELSIUS

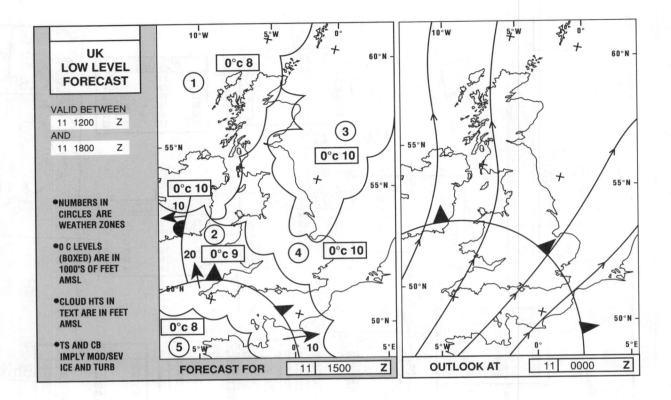

ZONE 1	GEN	8KM	NIL/RAIN	6/8ST 1000/1500 6-8/8LYR 2500/12000
	OCNL	4000M	RAIN	6/8ST 500/1500 8/8LYR 15000/19000
ZONE 2	GEN	10KM	NIL/RAIN	3-5/8SC 2000/4000 6/8LYR 8000/16000
	OCNL	4000M	RAIN	6/8ST 600/1500 8/8LYR 4000/20000
	ISOL	2000M	HEAVY RAIN/TS	5/8ST 400/1500 8/8LYR NS 3000/20000 +
				EMBD CB 5000/36000
				WITH SEV TURB AND ICE.
ZONE 3	GEN	3000M	MIST/DZ	8/8STSC 500/2500
	OCNL	0300M	FOG/DZ	8/8STSC 000/3000 3/8AC 7000/14000
ZONE 4	GEN	12KM	NIL	4-6/8AC 10000/14000
	LOC N	4000M	HAZE	4-6/8AC 10000/14000
	LOC S	8KM	NIL/RAIN	6/8AC 10000/16000
				SOME MTW ACTIVITY OVER ENGLAND
				AND WALES. MAX VSP 350 FPM AT 090.
ZONE 5	GEN	30KM	NIL	4-6/8CUSC 2500/5000
	OCNL	6KM	RAIN SH	5/8CU 2000/12000
	ISOL	4000M	HEAVY SH/TS	CB 1000/30000

OUTLOOK: UNTIL 11/0000Z:

1 There is a natural tendency for air to flow from areas of .... pressure to .... pressure

A High/high

B High/low

C Low/high

2 The pressure at sea level in the ISA is:

A 1012.35 mb

B 1025.13 mb

C 1013.25 mb

3 The lapse rate rate for a dry parcel of air is:

A 3°C/1000ft

B 1.5°C/1000ft

C 1.98°C/1000ft

4 In the northern hemisphere the coriolis effect deflects air to:

A The right

B The left

C Does not deflect the air at all

5 Select the true statement concerning isobars and wind flow patterns around high and low pressure systems that are shown on a pressure chart:

A Surface winds flow perpendicular to the isobars

B When the isobars are far apart, crests of standing waves may be marked by lenticular clouds

C When the isobars are close together, the pressure gradient force is stronger, and wind velocities are stronger.

6 With respect to high or low pressure systems:

A A high pressure area or ridge is an area of rising air

B A high pressure area or ridge is an area of descending air

C A low pressure area or trough is an area of descending air

7 What are the characteristics of a cold Airmass moving over a warm surface:

A Cumuloform clouds, turbulence, and good visibility.

B Cumuloform clouds, turbulence, and poor visibility.

C Stratiform clouds, smooth air, and poor visibility.

8 What is the term used to describe streamers of precipitation trailing beneath clouds, but evaporating before reaching the ground:

A Foehn

B Virga

C Dissipation trails

9 Cloud formed by turbulence and mixing is called:

A Stratus

B Roll cloud

C Turbulence cloud

10 Which weather phenomenon signals the beginning of the mature stage of a Thunderstorm:

A The appearance of an anvil top.

B Growth rate of cloud is maximum.

C The start of rain.

11 Thunderstorms are to be avoided by at least:

A 40 nm

B 10 nm

C 15 nm

12 Low level windshear is best described as:

A A change in windspeed and/or direction within a very short distance in the atmosphere.

B A downward motion of the air associated with continuous winds blowing with easterly component due to rotation of the earth.

C A violently rotating column of air extending from a CB.

13 In the northern hemisphere an aircraft flying from high to low pressure, will experience:

A No drift

B Port drift

C Starboard drift

14 A cold front moves _____ a warm front.

A Faster than

B Slower than

C The same speed as

15 The surface wind at midnight compared to the surface wind at midday:

A Backs and decreases

B Backs and increases

C Veers and decreases

16 Decode the following METAR for Amsterdam:

EHAM 12/0600 02025KT 3000 RA BKN005 OVC015 11/10 Q1012

A Amsterdam : Observation at 0600 Z, wind 020° at 25 knots, visibility 3000 metres in rain, cloud broken Stratus with base 500 ft. A.A.L. and 8 oktas Nimbostratus base 1500 ft. A.A.L. Temperature +11°C Dew point +10°C QNH 1012mb.

B Amsterdam : Observation at 0600 UTC, wind 020° at 25kts visibility 3000m with 6.1mm of rain, broken Stratus base 500ft above mean sea level, overcast Nimbostratus base 1500ft above mean sea level temperature +11°c Dewpoint +10°c QFE 1012mb

C Amsterdam : period valid between 0600 UTC and 0000 UTC wind 020° at 25kts 3000m in rain, broken of Stratus base 500ft above aerodrome level, 8 oktas Nimbostratus base 1500ft above aerodrome level, temperature between +10°c and +11°c QNH 1012mb

REFER TO LAPFORM THREE

17 What is significant about the warm front to the west of the Channel Islands?

A Warm front at the surface

B Warm Occlusion

C Warm front above the surface

18 Line 3, zone 2 cloud and turbulence:

A 8/8 nimbostratus 500 to 1600, moderate turbulence and moderate icing, locally severe icing

B Greater than 5 oktas of nimbostratus 500 to 10000 feet light turbulence and moderate airframe icing, locally severe turbulence

C 8 oktas nimbostratus, base 500 feet, tops 16000 feet with moderate turbulence and icing, locally severe icing

19 What is the 2000' wind at Lydd?

A 180/40

B 190/25

C 185/33

20 Decode zone 4, Line 2

A Isolated in the north of zone 4, visibility 300 metres in rain and drizzle, 6 oktas stratus base 5000 feet tops 12000 feet, 6 oktas stratus base 2500 feet tops 16000 feet with moderate turbulence and icing.

B Isolated in the north of zone 4, visibility 3000 metres in rain and drizzle, 6 oktas stratus base 500 feet tops 1200 feet, 6 oktas stratus base 2500 feet tops 16000 feet with moderate turbulence and icing.

C Isolated north of zone 4, visibility 3000 metres in rain and drizzle, 6 oktas stratus base 500 feet tops 1200 feet, 6 oktas stratus base 2500 feet tops 16000 feet with moderate turbulence and icing.

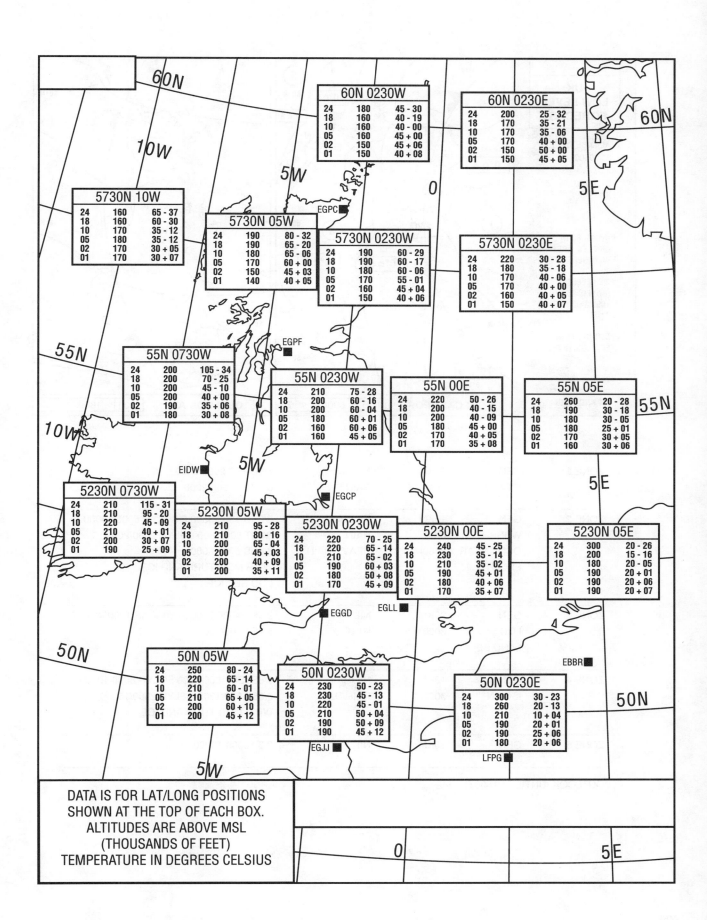

DATA IS FOR LAT/LONG POSITIONS
SHOWN AT THE TOP OF EACH BOX.
ALTITUDES ARE ABOVE MSL
(THOUSANDS OF FEET)
TEMPERATURE IN DEGREES CELSIUS

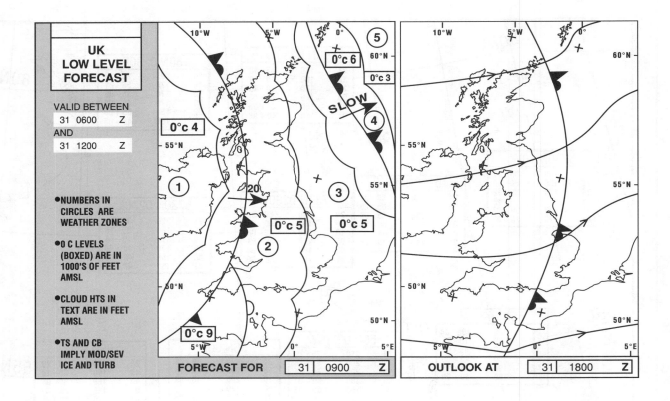

ZONE 1	GEN	30KM	NIL	6/8CUSC 2000/6000
	ISOL W	8KM	RAIN SH	6/8CU 1500/12000

ZONE 2	GEN	15KM	NIL/RAIN	5/8SC 1500/3500 6-8/8LYR 5000/18000
	WDSPR	6KM	RAIN	6/8ST 800/1500 8/8LYR 2000/20000
	OCNL NEAR	3000M	HEAVY RAIN	8/8NS 500/16000
	FRONTS			WITH MOD TURB AND ICE.
				LOC SEV ICE

ZONE 3	GEN	20KM	NIL	2/8SC 4000/7000 2-6/8ACAS 12000/15000
	LOC	3000M	MIST	5/8ST 500/1000
	LAND SE			

ZONE 4	GEN	12KM	NIL/RAIN	6/8STSC 1000/6000 5/8LYR 8000/10000
	ISOL N	3000M	RAIN/DZ	6/8ST 500/1200 6/8LYR 2500/16000
				WITH MOD TURB AND ICE

ZONE 5	GEN	15KM	NIL	3/8 10000/12000

OUTLOOK: UNTIL 31/1800Z:

1 When a north-westerly airflow is reaching the UK, which of the following is most likely to be true?

A It is a Tropical Maritime air mass from the Azores

B It is a Polar Continental air mass from Scandinavia

C It is a Polar Maritime airmass from the north Atlantic/Arctic

2 A sea breeze blows:

A From the sea by day.

B From the sea by night.

C From the land by day.

3 As a warm front passes the weather is:

A Slight showers -> Moderate continuous drizzle.

B Moderate continuous rain -> Intermittent slight drizzle.

C Moderate continuous rain -> Rain showers.

4 The cloud sequence associated with the passage of a cold front is:

A CU/CB -> Isolated CU/SC

B ST/SC -> CU/SC

C NS/ST -> AC/AS

5 Moist air is:

A Denser than dry air.

B Warmer than dry air.

C Less dense than dry air.

6 Cloud bases in TAF's and METAR's are given in:

A Heights AMSL

B Heights above official aerodrome level.

C Heights above 1013 mb pressure level.

7 Tropical maritime air brings to the UK:

A ST cloud and rain.

B ST/SC cloud and drizzle.

C CU/SC and showers.

8 You are flying in a layer of haze, late on a winter afternoon. Which of the following statements is true?

A Flight visibility into sun will be worse

B Flight visibility 'down sun' will be worse

C The position of the sun will not effect flight visibility

9 The lowest in-flight visibility is likely to be encountered in:

A   Rain below nimbostratus clouds.

B   Showers below cumulus clouds.

C   Drizzle below stratus clouds.

10 In relation to mountain wave activity, which of the following cloud types signifies the most turbulent conditions?

A   Roll or rotor clouds

B   Lenticular clouds

C   Stratiform cloud covering the mountain tops

11 Carburettor icing is unlikely:

A   In cloud.

B   At temperatures between -10°C and -30°C.

C   When the relative humidity is 40%.

12 The wind which results from air warming on the side of a hill is known as:

A   A valley wind.

B   An anabatic wind.

C   A katabatic wind.

13 An environmental lapse rate is observed to be 2.5°C/1000 ft, which of the following is correct:

A   A dry parcel of air would be stable if it was forced to rise.

B   A saturated parcel of air would be stable if it was forced to rise.

C   A dry parcel of air would be unstable if it was forced to rise.

14 As a warm front approaches, the cloud base:

A   Remains the same.

B   Lowers.

C   Rises.

15 The general visibility associated with a cold front _____ the visibility associated with a warm front.

A   Is worse than.

B   Is the same as.

C   Is better than.

16 A V-shaped extension of a low pressure area is called a:

A   Ridge

B   Col

C   Trough

REFER TO LAPFORM 4

17 Your fax machine failed to print the cloud type in zone 5. What is the most likely answer?

A Altocumulus

B Cumulonimbus

C Nimbostratus

18 What is the altitude of the 0°C isotherm off the southern coast of Cornwall?

A 5500'

B 9000'

C 550m

19 Zone 3 top line:

A 2 oktas Stratocumulus base 400' top's 700' 2-6 oktas Altocumulus or Altostratus 1200'/1500'

B 2 oktas Stratocumulus 4000' to 2000', 2-6 oktas Altocumulus or Altostratus 1200'/1500'

C 2 oktas Stratocumulus 4000' to 7000' 2-6 oktas Altocumulus or Altostratus 12000' to 15000'

20 What is the 2000' wind at EGPF?

A 155/55

B 160/60

C 155/50

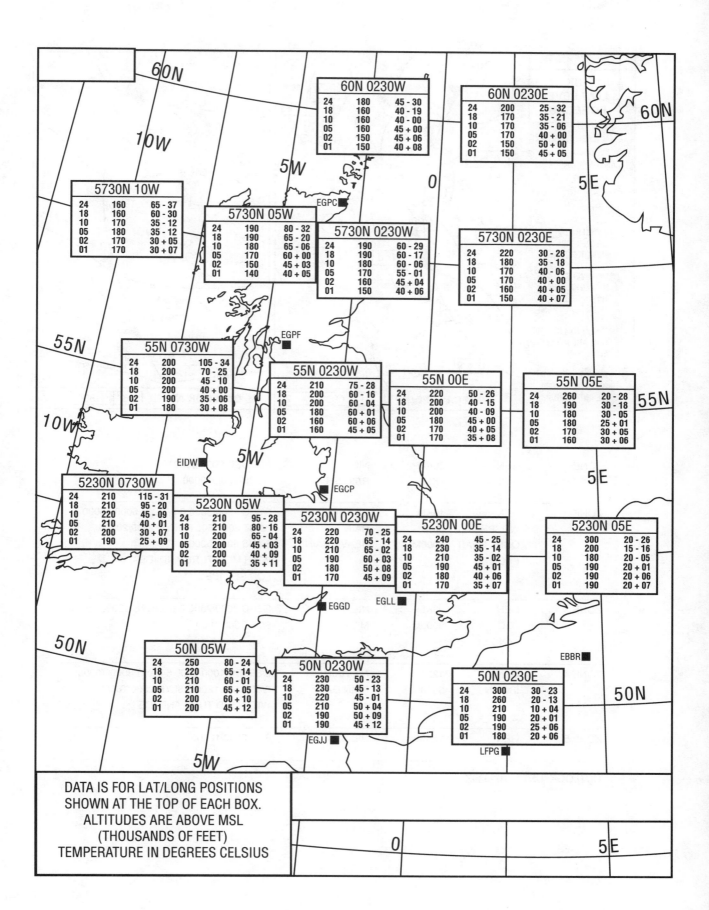

DATA IS FOR LAT/LONG POSITIONS SHOWN AT THE TOP OF EACH BOX. ALTITUDES ARE ABOVE MSL (THOUSANDS OF FEET) TEMPERATURE IN DEGREES CELSIUS

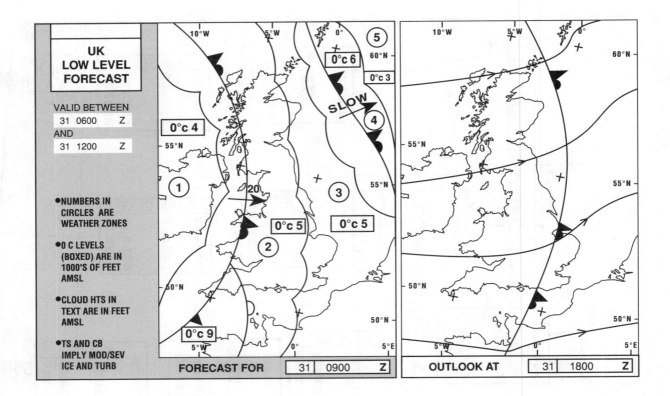

ZONE 1	GEN	30KM	NIL	6/8CUSC 2000/6000
	ISOL W	8KM	RAIN SH	6/8CU 1500/12000
ZONE 2	GEN	15KM	NIL/RAIN	5/8SC 1500/3500 6-8/8LYR 5000/18000
	WDSPR	6KM	RAIN	6/8ST 800/1500 8/8LYR 2000/20000
	OCNL NEAR	3000M	HEAVY RAIN	8/8NS 500/16000
	FRONTS			WITH MOD TURB AND ICE.
				LOC SEV ICE
ZONE 3	GEN	20KM	NIL	2/8SC 4000/7000 2-6/8ACAS 12000/15000
	LOC	3000M	MIST	5/8ST 500/1000
	LAND SE			
ZONE 4	GEN	12KM	NIL/RAIN	6/8STSC 1000/6000 5/8LYR 8000/10000
	ISOL N	3000M	RAIN/DZ	6/8ST 500/1200 6/8LYR 2500/16000
				WITH MOD TURB AND ICE
ZONE 5	GEN	15KM	NIL	3/8 10000/12000

OUTLOOK: UNTIL 31/1800Z:

1 A mountain range runs north-south, and a strong wind is blowing from the west. What meteorological phenomena is most likely and where will it be at its most dangerous?

A Fog; in the valleys

B Mountain wave activity; to the west of the mountains

C Mountain wave activity; to the east of the mountains

2 Oxygen percentage of the atmosphere is:

A 87%

B 21%

C 78%

3 A parcel of air is said to be saturated if it has a relative humidity of:

A 50%

B 100%

C Greater than 90%

4 Heating from solar radiation is greatest in the:

A Tropics

B Temperate Zones

C Poles

5 The earths surface reaches its maximum temperature around:

A 12:00

B 11:00

C 15:00

6 If you stand with your back to the wind in the northern hemisphere, the low pressure will be:

A On your Left

B On your Right

C Behind

7 The wind at the surface is 240/15 kts what will it be at 2000':

A 220/25 kts

B 260/25 kts

C 280/15 kts

8 High level cloud has a base of _____ and is termed _____ .

A 15,000'/Nimbus

B 20,000'/Cumuliform

C 20,000'/Cirriform

9 Water vapour (GAS) Changes directly to ice (SOLID). This is called _____ and
_____ Latent Heat:

A Sublimation / Releases

B Deposition / Releases

C Condensation / Absorbs

10 The temperature at which a parcel of air becomes saturated if it cools is called:

A Dewpoint Temperature

B Saturation Temperature

C Condensation Temperature

11 The saturated adiabatic lapse rate (SALR) is approximately:

A 3.00°C/1000ft

B 1.98°C/1000ft

C 1.5°C/1000ft

12 Continuous rain is associated with which type of cloud?

A Nimbostratus

B Cumulus

C Stratus

13 In the cumulus or building stage of a thunderstorm there are:

A Updrafts only

B Downdrafts only

C Updrafts and downdrafts

14 During the mature stage of a thunderstorm the heaviest fall of rain or hail occurs in:

A The first 30 mins

B The first 5 mins

C The last 10 mins

15 Polar maritime air is:

A Cold, Moist, Stable

B Cold, Dry, Unstable

C Cold, Moist, Unstable

16 The following denotes:

A A cold front at the surface

B A warm front at the surface

C A warm front at 10,000ft AMSL

REFER TO LAPFORM FIVE

17 The front between Wales and the North East Coast is a:

A Warm occlusion

B Quasi stationary front at the surface

C Cold occlusion

18 What is the approximate surface wind at EGGD?

A 290/10

B 250/20

C 245/10

19 Assuming a distance of 60nm, at what time will the cold front reach the Isle of Wight?

A 12:00 BST

B 12:00 UTC

C 10:30 UTC

20 Zone 2 bottom line EMBD CB 020/280.

A May be ignored as the forecast cloud base is below 2000'

B Can be seen and avoided

C Is particularly hazardous

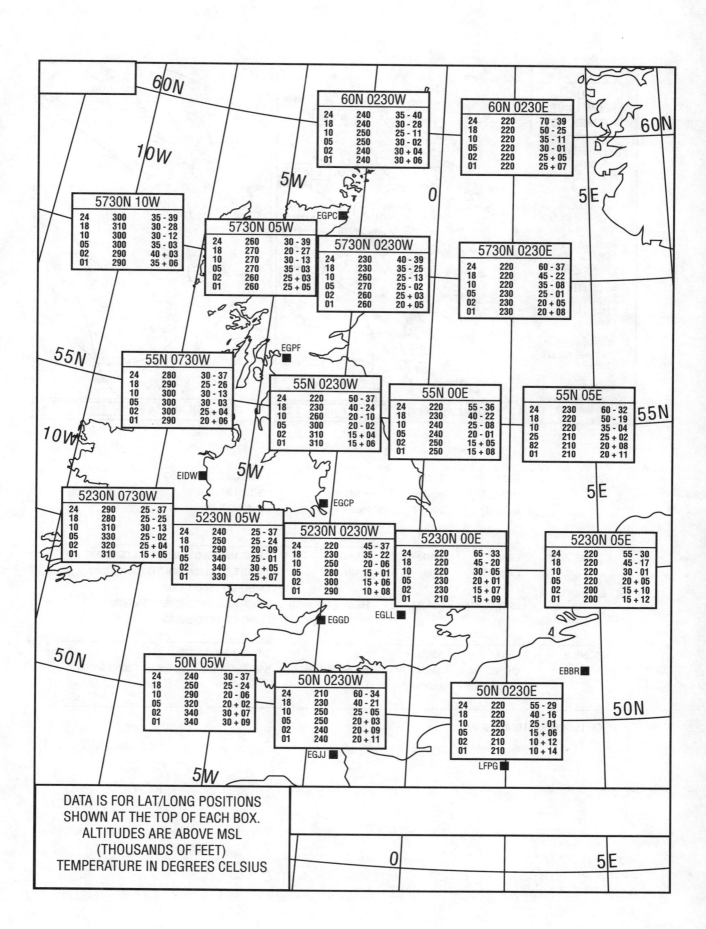

DATA IS FOR LAT/LONG POSITIONS
SHOWN AT THE TOP OF EACH BOX.
ALTITUDES ARE ABOVE MSL
(THOUSANDS OF FEET)
TEMPERATURE IN DEGREES CELSIUS

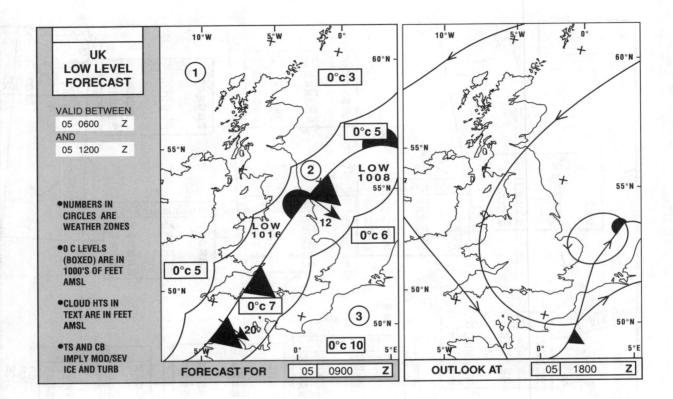

ZONE 1	GEN	30KM	NIL	4-6/8CUSC 2000/6000
	OCNL	20KM	RAIN SH	6/8CU 1500/10000
	ISOL N	3000M	HEAVY SH /TS/HAIL	CB 800/20000

ZONE 2	GEN	15KM	RAIN	5/8SC 1500/6000 6/8LYR 10000/20000
	OCNL	6KM	RAIN	3-6/8ST 800/1200 8/8LYR 2000/18000 EMBD CU 1500/10000
	ISOL FRONT	2000M	HEAVY RAIN/TS	5/8ST 300/1200 8/8NS 1500/18000 EMBD CB 2000/28000

ZONE 3	GEN	30KM	NIL	2-5/8SC 2000/5000
	OCNL NW	20KM	NIL/RAIN	5/8STSC 1500/5000 5/8AC 12000/18000
	LOC LAND	5000M	HAZE	

OUTLOOK: UNTIL 05/1900Z:

1 The weather charts show a warm front approaching your intended departure airfield at a rate of 20 knots. It started raining at the departure airfield at 0600, and the time now is 1000. At what time, approximately, do you expect the passage of the front?

A 1200

B 1600

C 2000

2 Air density generally _____ as altitude increases:

A Increases

B Decreases

C Stays the same.

3 You are flying at a constant indicated altitude of 2000 feet with a QNH set of 1015. After a long flight towards a low pressure area without up-dating the pressure setting, a new QNH of 998 mb is passed to you. When this is set on the altimeter what is the new indicated altitude (assume 1 mb = 30 feet) ?

A 1490 feet

B 2490 feet

C 2000 feet

4 An inversion means that the temperature _____ as altitude increases:

A Decreases

B Increases

C Stays the same.

5 The approximate temperature lapse rate in the ISA is ____ degrees C per 1000 feet:

A 3.0°C

B 1.5°C

C 2.0°C

6 What prevents air from flowing directly from high to low pressure areas?

A Coriolis force.

B Surface friction.

C Pressure gradient force.

7 The general circulation of air associated with a high pressure area in the northern hemisphere is:

A Inward, downward and counter clockwise.

B Outward, upward and clockwise.

C Outward, downward and clockwise.

8 Low land areas to the east of high ground are sometimes referred to as having a 'rain shadow'. This means:

A In the prevailing westerly winds, more precipitation tends to fall in the 'rain shadow' area.

B Most precipitation tends to fall on the up-wind slopes of the high ground.

C By a statistical freak, 'rain shadow' areas get less precipitation for no clearly defined reason.

9 The backing of the surface wind is greater over:

A Polar regions.

B Sea

C Land

10 What determines the structure or type of clouds which will form as a result of air being forced to ascend:

A The stability of the air before lifting occurs.

B The method by which air is lifted.

C The relative humidity of the air after lifting occurs.

11 The presence of standing lenticular Altocumulus clouds is a good indication of:

A Very strong turbulence

B An approaching storm

C Heavy icing conditions

12 The hazards that thunderstorms pose to aviation are:

A Windshear, severe turbulence, hail

B Heavy showers, lightning, severe icing

C Both 'A' & 'B'

13 The conditions associated with anticyclones are:

A Moderate or poor visibility - no convective cloud of any extent

B Fair weather cumulus - light winds

C Stratus and drizzle - advection fog

14 It is October, and an area of high pressure has been established over the UK for several days. Which of the following is most likely to represent the TAF for a Midlands airport?

A 0716 04025KT 7000 BKN013 OVC090=

B 0716 05004KT 0800 FG OVC001 TEMPO 0709 0200 VV/// BECMG 0811 3000   BR OVC005 TEMPO 1116 6000 SCT007=

C 0716 30005KT 9999 SCT035 PROB30 TEMPO 0710 5000 TSRA BKN050CB=

15 The cloud sequence expected from a warm front is:

A CI, AS, NS, ST

B AS, CI, CS, ST, NS

C CI, CS, AS, NS, ST

16 On a cool and cloudless night with no wind, and the air in contact with the surface cooled to it's dewpoint temperature (Say - 5°C), which of the following is most likely to form?

A DEW

B FOG

C FROST

REFER TO LAPFORM 6

17 What is the least forecast visibility in zone 3?

A 1500m

B 200m or less

C 5km

18 Reference zone 3 line 2; which area is being referred to?

A Overcast near front

B Occasionally ahead of zone 3 boundary

C Occasionally near front

19 What is the 2000' wind at EBBR?

A 260/25 gusting to 37

B 270/15

C 265/20

20 Zone 1 3rd line; 6/8ACAS 10000/18000 means:

A 6 oktas Altocumulus/Altostratus base 10000 feet, tops 18000 feet

B 6 oktas Altocumulus/Altostratus base 1000 feet, tops 1800 feet

C 6 oktas Altocumulus/Altostratus base either 10000 feet or 18000 feet

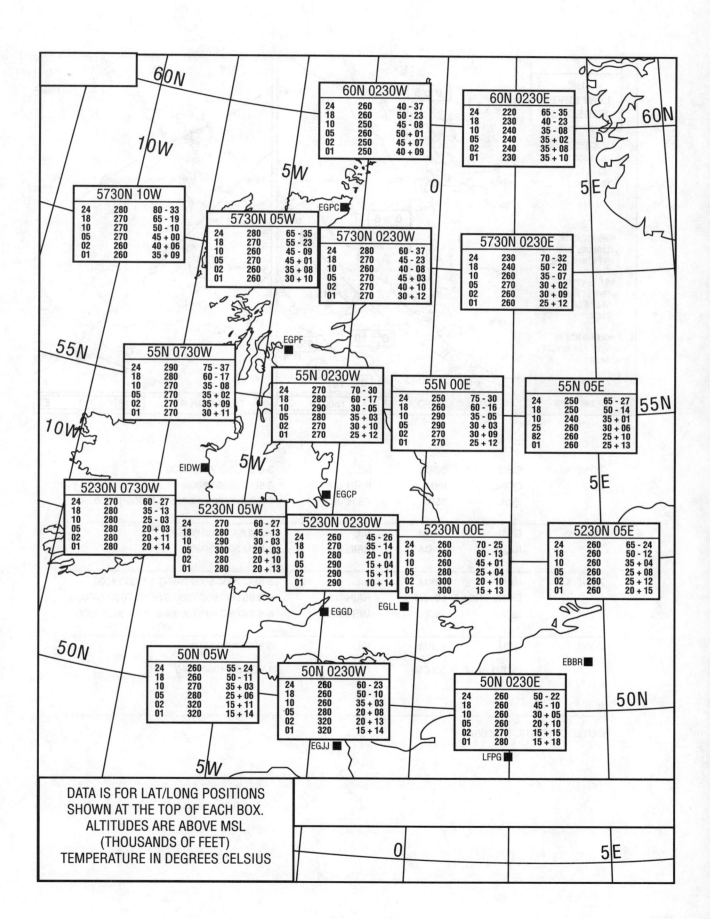

DATA IS FOR LAT/LONG POSITIONS
SHOWN AT THE TOP OF EACH BOX.
ALTITUDES ARE ABOVE MSL
(THOUSANDS OF FEET)
TEMPERATURE IN DEGREES CELSIUS

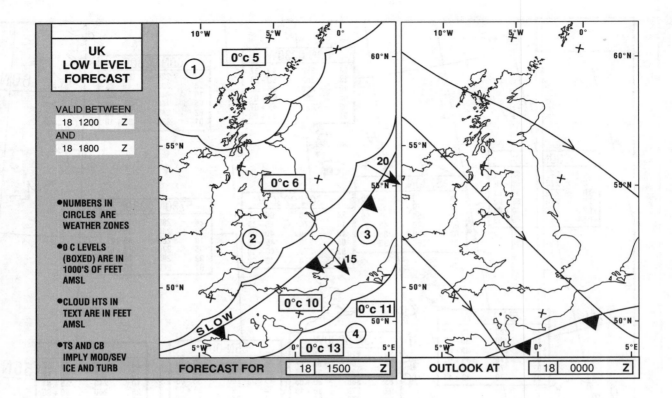

UK LOW LEVEL FORECAST
VALID BETWEEN
18 1200 Z
AND
18 1800 Z

- NUMBERS IN CIRCLES ARE WEATHER ZONES
- 0 C LEVELS (BOXED) ARE IN 1000'S OF FEET AMSL
- CLOUD HTS IN TEXT ARE IN FEET AMSL
- TS AND CB IMPLY MOD/SEV ICE AND TURB

FORECAST FOR 18 1500 Z

OUTLOOK AT 18 0000 Z

ZONE 1	GEN	30KM	NIL	3-6/8CUSC 2200/8000
	OCNL	8KM	RAIN SH	6/8CU 1500/12000
	ISOL	3500	TS/HAIL	CB 800/25000 6/8ACAS 10000/18000

ZONE 2	GEN	35KM	NIL	3/8CUSC 3000/6000
	ISOL	10KM	RAIN SH	6/8CU 2000/9000

ZONE 3	GEN	20KM	NIL	5/8SC 2500/6000 2/8AC 12000/14000
	OCNL FRONT	5000M	RAIN/DZ	6-8/8STSC 800/7000 6/8LYR 7000/14000
	ISOL	1500M	MIST/DZ	6-8/8STSC 400/7000 6/8LYR 7000/14000

ZONE 4	GEN	15KM	NIL	5/8SC 3000/5500
	ISOL LAND	5000M	HAZE	1/8CUSC 4000/5500

OUTLOOK: UNTIL 18/0000Z:

1 Which of the following statements is true of advection fog:

A It can occur over land and sea

B It occurs in valleys and over rivers at night

C It can occur when dry air moves over a warm surface

2 The rate of fall of pressure with height is:

A Greater in warm air than cold air

B Greater in cold air than warm air

C The same for cold or warm air

3 You are flying below 1000 feet AGL in precipitation ahead of a warm front in winter. The outside air temperature is -2 degrees C. What of the following meteorological phenomena is most likely to affect the aircraft ?

A Rain ice

B Hail

C Radiation fog

4 The surface temperature is +20 degrees C, the dewpoint is +5 degrees C. What is the most likely height for the base of cumulus cloud?

A 7000 feet

B 2000 feet

C 500 feet

5 The average change of pressure with height in the lower levels of the atmosphere is:

A 1mb/20ft

B 1mb/30ft

C 1mb/50ft

6 On a cold clear night, ice crystals can form on a surface directly from water vapour. This process is known as:

A Sublimation

B Supercooling

C Supersaturation

7 In the northern hemisphere, the surface winds in an anticyclone blow:

A Clockwise and backed from the isobars

B Clockwise and veered from the isobars

C Anticlockwise and backed from the isobars

8 Temperature in the ISA decreases by ....°C for each 1000ft gained.

A 2°C

B 1.98°C

C 1.9°C

9 The wind which results from air cooling on the side of a valley is called:

A A valley wind

B A katabatic wind

C An anabatic wind

10 If you stand facing the wind in the northern hemisphere the low pressure area is:

A Left

B Right

C In front of you

11 As the parcel of air rises, it cools and its ability to hold water vapour:

A Increases

B Decreases

C Remains the same.

Refer to the following diagram, complete the diagram and answer questions 12 to 14.

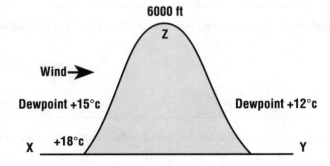

Using the standard lapse rates sketch in the cloud due to the FÖHN wind effect.

12 What is the temperature at Z?

A 0°C

B +7.5°C

C +6°C

13 What is the temperature at Y?

A +21°C

B +18°C

C +15°C

14 State the requirements in terms of humidity and stability for the FÖHN wind to occur.

A Moist, Stable

B Dry, Stable

C Moist, Unstable

15 The precipitation associated with a cold front usually extends horizontally approximately

A 50-100 nm

B 200-300 nm

C 500-600 nm

16 Considering the passage of a polar frontal depression, what cloud types would you expect at the warm front?

A CI, AS

B NS, ST

C ST, SC

REFER TO LAPFORM 7

17 What is the mean speed of the cold front crossing Cornwall?

A 25 kts

B 15 kts

C 15 mph

18 What type of turbulence and icing can we expect from zone 1, line 3?

A Moderate icing, severe turbulence

B Moderate icing, moderate turbulence

C Severe icing, severe turbulence

19 A coastal airfield in which zone and specific line might report the following METAR: EG?? 18/1020 30020KT 1200 BR BKN005

A Zone 2 line 4

B Zone 1 line 3

C Zone 3 line 4

20 Zone 2, last line. What visibility can we expect?

A 2000m

B 200m or less

C 500m

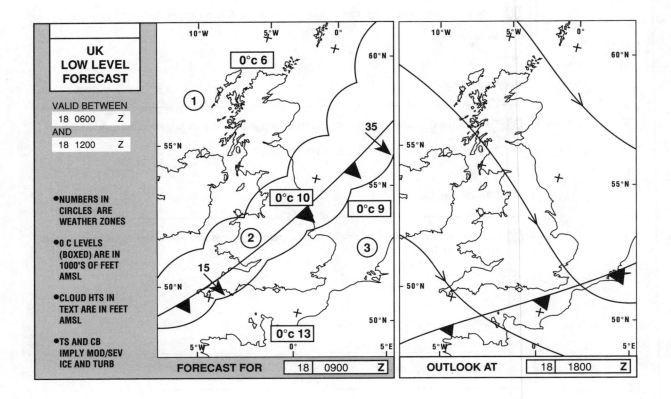

ZONE 1	GEN	25KM	NIL	4-6/8CUSC 2500/5000
	OCNL	8KM	RAIN SH	6/8CU 1000/10000
	ISOL N	3500	TS/HAIL	CB 800/25000 6/8AC 10000/18000
ZONE 2	GEN	20KM	NIL	5/8SC 2500/6000 6/8AC 10000/18000
	OCNL	10KM	RAIN	6/8STSC 1000/7500 8/8AC 8000/20000
	ISOL	3000M	HEAVY RAIN	8/8NS 500/16000
	LOC	2000	MIST/DZ	6/8ST 500/1500 6/8LYR 1800/18000
ZONE 3	GEN	25KM	NIL	NIL-2/8SC 3000/4500
	ISOL W	15KM	NIL/RAIN	NIL-2/8SC 3000/4500 5/8AC12000/18000
	ISOL LAND	5000M	HAZE	NIL-2/8ST 800/1500
	OCNL SEA/ COT	1500M	MIST	5/8ST 500/1500

OUTLOOK: UNTIL 18/1800Z:

1 The Tropopause is:

A The layer of the atmosphere nearest the earth's surface.

B The second layer nearest to the earth's surface.

C The boundary between the first and second layers.

2 1225 g/m^3 relates to :

A The air density at sea level in the ISA

B The air pressure at sea level in the ISA

C The air density at 10000 feet in ISA conditions

3 The surface temperature is +15°C, the base of some cumulus cloud is 4000 feet. What is the most likely value for the dewpoint ?

A + 10 degrees C

B - 6 degrees C

C + 6 degrees C

4 The approximate height of the tropopause above mean sea level in the ISA is:

A 65,000ft

B 36,000ft

C 82,000ft

5 The temperature at 10,000ft in the ISA is:

A -5°C

B -10°C

C -15°C

6 The amount of water vapour that air can hold is determined by its:

A Pressure

B Temperature

C Dewpoint

7 The dry adiabatic lapse rate (DALR) in the atmosphere is:

A 1.98°C/1000ft

B 1.5°C/1000ft

C 3°C/1000ft

8 The observed temperature at the surface is +13°C and at 4000ft it is +6°C. The state of the atmosphere can be described as:

A Stable

B Unstable

C Mixed

MET 43

9 If an aircraft is flying towards an area of low pressure (in the northern hemisphere) what drift, if any, would it experience?

A Starboard

B None

C Port

10 The force that causes a parcel of air to start moving from an area of high pressure to an area of low pressure, is called?

A Gradient force

B Coriolis force

C Pressure gradient force

11 If the 2000ft wind is 310/35 and the surface wind over land is 280/20, what is the surface wind likely to be over the sea?

A 270/15

B 295/25

C 280/20

12 A strong wind flow over a mountain range which causes strong downcurrents on the Lee side may be marked by:

A Cirrus

B Lenticularis

C Stratus

13 You are approaching an active Cumulonimbus cloud. Which of the following courses of action is valid?

A You can fly around the CB, avoiding it by least 10 miles

B You must land immediately and wait for the CB to pass over

C You can fly under the CB if you can see through to other side

14 At an airfield you ask for a TAF, and are given the following from the fax:
EIDW 0716 12005KT 0100 FG BKN001 BECMG 0810 8000 NSW
Why should you not accept this TAF?

A Because the weather is dreadful.

B Because the TAF is not complete.

C Because the cloud group has been incorrectly transmitted.

15 Orographic clouds form:

A Over the sea during the winter months

B Whenever the eddying motion associated with mechanical turbulence sets off large scale vertical movements

C Over mountain ranges, large hills or sloping planes

16 Which of the following is most likely to "trigger off" a cumulonimbus:

A Convergence in tropical latitudes

B Subsidence in tropical latitudes.

C Convection in polar latitudes

17 If maritime air is heated from below as it moves from its source region it will become:

A Stable

B Unstable

C Neutrally stable

18 A CB with anvil signifies that the thunderstorm is in:

A The building stage

B The mature stage

C The decaying stage

19 Approaching Cirrus cloud may signify:

A An approaching warm front

B An approaching cold front

C Severe turbulence and icing conditions

20 Density at the surface will be low when:

A Pressure is high and temperature is high

B Pressure is low and temperature is low

C Pressure is low and temperature is high

1 Which of the following statements best describes the change in pressure with the passage of typical warm and cold fronts:

A After warm front steadily falling, after cold front steady

B After warm front steadies, after cold front rises quickly

C After warm front rises, after cold front falls

2 Clouds formed by convection will always:

A Be layer clouds

B Be Cu, Cb or Ns

C Have rising cloud tops and may develop into Cb as the day progresses

3 Moist, stable air with a surface temperature of +15°C is forced to rise over a range of hills, mean height 5000ft. If the air remains stable and the cloud base is at 2000ft on the windward side, and 4000ft on the Lee side, what will be the Lee side surface temperature?

A +12°C

B +15°C

C +18°C

4 On a particular day, the temperature at 6000 feet is +7°C. In relation to ISA conditions:

A The temperature at 6000 feet is less than ISA

B The temperature at 6000 feet is greater than ISA

C The temperature at 6000 feet is equal to ISA

5 A METAR includes the abbreviation 'CAVOK'. Which of the following might exist at the time of the METAR without invalidating the terms of this abbreviation.

A Total cloud cover at 6000 feet

B 1/8 of CB at 25000

C Visibility of 9999 m

6 Gust fronts are associated with:

A Standing waves

B Thunderstorms

C High pressure areas

7 Advection fog is most likely to form when:

A Dry, warm air moves over a cold sea causing evaporation and consequent condensation

B Warm, moist air moves across a cold sea surface and is cooled to saturation temperature

C Warm, moist air moves across a cold land surface and is cooled to below its dewpoint

8 As air rises, it cools by:

A Conductive mixing

B Adiabatic expansion

C Loss of height by long wave radiation

9 Diurnal variation of temperature over land in mid latitudes is:

A Hottest at 1400 UTC, coolest at sunrise

B Hottest at 1500 LMT, coolest at sunrise

C Hottest at noon, coolest at sunset

10 In the ISA, the temperature is assumed to decrease at a rate of:

A 1.98°C per 1000 ft

B 1.98°C per 1000 metres

C 2K per 1000 ft

11 In a TAF the abbreviation BECMG indicates:

A An expected permanent change in forecast conditions

B Becalmed conditions at an offshore installation

C The time of a temporary change in weather conditions

12 When a wind changes direction from southerly to south westerly, it is said to:

A Veer in the northern hemisphere & back in the southern hemisphere

B Back in the northern hemisphere & veer in the southern hemisphere

C Veer in either hemisphere

13 As a cold front passes the pressure:

A Falls

B Rises

C Remains constant

14 Ice forms over the static vent of an aircraft and blocks it during the climb, the altimeter will read:

A Zero

B Correctly

C A constant altitude

15 Decode the following TAF for Lydd:
EGMD 03/12-21 24015G25KT 6000 BKN035 TEMPO 5000 SHRA BKN020

A Lydd, date 03 period of validity 1200 to 2100 UTC. Surface wind 240 degrees 15 knots going to be 25 knots. Visibility 6000 metres. Cloud 5 to 7 oktas base 3500 feet AMSL, temporarily visibility 5000 metres in rain showers, cloud 5 to 7 oktas base 2000 feet AMSL.

B Lydd, date 03 period of validity 1200 to 2100 UTC. Surface wind 240 degrees 15 knots gusting 25 knots. Visibility 6000 metres. Cloud 1 to 4 oktas base 3500 feet AAL, temporarily visibility 5000 metres in rain showers, cloud 1 to 4 oktas base 2000 feet AAL.

C Lydd, date 03 period of validity 1200 to 2100 UTC. Surface wind 240 degrees 15 knots gusting 25 knots. Visibility 6000 metres. Cloud 5 to 7 oktas base 3500 feet AAL, temporarily visibility 5000 metres in rain showers, cloud 5 to 7 oktas base 2000 feet AAL.

16 In a metar the decode for hail is:

A GR

B HA

C PE

NOW REFER TO LAPFORM 9

17 Your FAX machine did not print the cloud type zone 2 line 2 what is the most likely answer:

A Cumulonimbus

B Cumulus

C Altostratus

18 Freezing level in zone 4 is:

A 1000'

B 100'

C 10,000'

19 What is the lowest forecast visibility in zone 3?

A 200m or less

B 800m

C 3500m

20 What is the worst forecast weather for the Kent coast at 1700UTC

A 20km nil weather. Scattered strato cumulus 3000' to 6000'

B 800m fog - drizzle. 8/8 stratus/ strato cumulus 200'/ 5000' moderate turbulence and ice.

C 4000m heavy showers thunderstorms hail cumulonimbus 800'/20000' severe icing and turbulence.

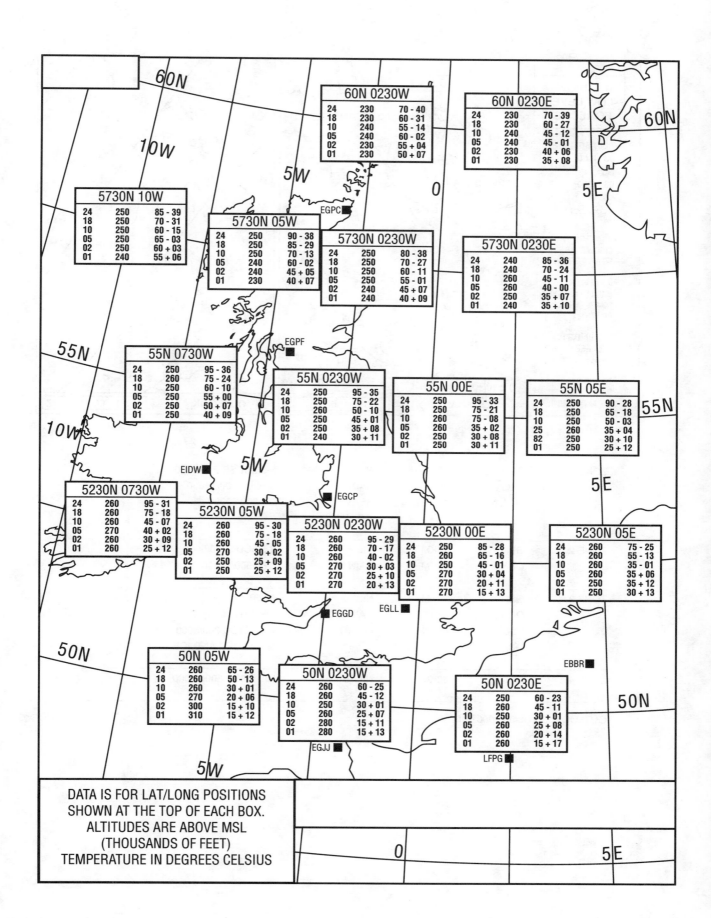

60N 0230W

24	230	70 - 40
18	230	60 - 31
10	240	55 - 14
05	240	60 - 02
02	230	55 + 04
01	230	50 + 07

60N 0230E

24	230	70 - 39
18	230	60 - 27
10	240	45 - 12
05	240	45 - 01
02	230	40 + 06
01	230	35 + 08

5730N 10W

24	250	85 - 39
18	250	70 - 31
10	250	60 - 15
05	250	65 - 03
02	250	60 + 03
01	240	55 + 06

5730N 05W

24	250	90 - 38
18	250	85 - 29
10	250	70 - 13
05	240	60 - 02
02	240	45 + 05
01	230	40 + 07

5730N 0230W

24	250	80 - 38
18	250	70 - 27
10	250	60 - 11
05	250	55 - 01
02	240	45 + 07
01	240	40 + 09

5730N 0230E

24	240	85 - 36
18	240	70 - 24
10	260	45 - 11
05	260	40 - 00
02	250	35 + 07
01	240	35 + 10

55N 0730W

24	250	95 - 36
18	260	75 - 24
10	250	60 - 10
05	250	55 + 00
02	250	50 + 07
01	250	40 + 09

55N 0230W

24	250	95 - 35
18	250	75 - 22
10	260	50 - 10
05	250	45 + 01
02	250	35 + 08
01	240	30 + 11

55N 00E

24	250	95 - 33
18	250	75 - 21
10	260	75 - 08
05	260	35 + 02
02	260	30 + 08
01	250	30 + 11

55N 05E

24	250	90 - 28
18	250	65 - 18
10	250	50 - 03
25	260	35 + 04
82	250	30 + 10
01	250	25 + 12

5230N 0730W

24	260	95 - 31
18	260	75 - 18
10	260	45 - 07
05	270	40 + 02
02	260	30 + 09
01	260	25 + 12

5230N 05W

24	260	95 - 30
18	260	75 - 18
10	260	45 - 05
05	270	30 + 02
02	250	25 + 09
01	250	25 + 12

5230N 0230W

24	260	95 - 29
18	260	70 - 17
10	260	40 - 02
05	270	30 + 03
02	270	25 + 10
01	270	20 + 13

5230N 00E

24	250	85 - 28
18	260	65 - 16
10	250	45 - 01
05	270	30 + 04
02	270	20 + 11
01	270	15 + 13

5230N 05E

24	260	75 - 25
18	260	55 - 13
10	260	35 - 01
05	260	35 + 06
02	250	35 + 12
01	250	30 + 13

50N 05W

24	260	65 - 26
18	260	50 - 13
10	260	30 + 01
05	270	20 + 06
02	300	15 + 10
01	310	15 + 12

50N 0230W

24	260	60 - 25
18	260	45 - 12
10	250	30 + 01
05	260	25 + 07
02	280	15 + 11
01	280	15 + 13

50N 0230E

24	250	60 - 23
18	260	45 - 11
10	250	30 + 01
05	260	25 + 08
02	260	20 + 14
01	260	15 + 17

DATA IS FOR LAT/LONG POSITIONS
SHOWN AT THE TOP OF EACH BOX.
ALTITUDES ARE ABOVE MSL
(THOUSANDS OF FEET)
TEMPERATURE IN DEGREES CELSIUS

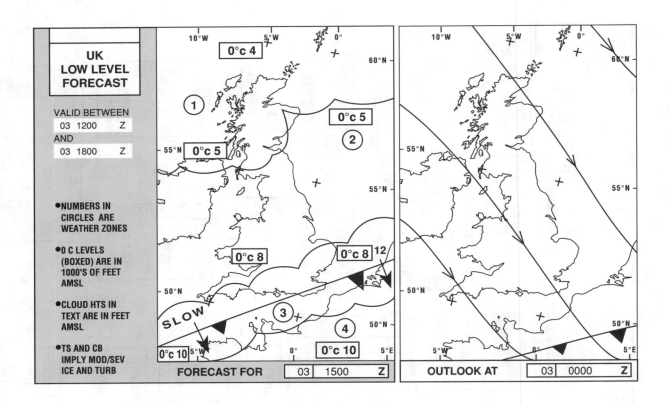

ZONE 1	GEN	30KM	NIL	3-6/8CUSC 2000/8000
	FRQ	8KM	RAIN SH	6/8CU 1200/14000
	ISOL N	4000M	HEAVY SH /TS/HAIL	CB 800/20000

ZONE 2	GEN	30KM	NIL	3-5/8CU 2500/6000
	OCNL	10KM	RAIN SH	6/8 1500/10000

ZONE 3	GEN	10KM	NIL/RAIN	5/8ST 1200/1500 6-8/8LYR 2000/8000
	OCNL	3500M	RAIN DZ	8/8LYR 600/10000
	LOC	0800M	FOG/DZ	4-6/8STSC 200/5000
	OCNL			MOD TURB AND ICE

ZONE 4	GEN	20KM	NIL/RAIN	NIL-1/8SC 3000/6000

OUTLOOK: UNTIL 03/0000Z:

1 The temperature at sea level in the ISA is:

A   +10.13°C

B   +15°F

C   +15°C

2 A land breeze blows:

A   From the sea by day.

B   From the land by night.

C   From the land by day.

3 In an anticyclone, the air mass tends to:

A   Ascend and warm.

B   Subside and cool.

C   Subside and warm.

4 In a typical depression:

A   The warm front moves faster than the cold front.

B   The warm front moves slower than the cold front.

C   The cold front moves slower than the warm front.

5 _____ air is associated with high pressure.

A   Subsiding

B   Rising

C   Stagnant

6 For carburettor ice to form, the outside air must be:

A   Cold and moist

B   Moist

C   Below freezing

7 If radiation fog forms on a clear night with light winds, an increase in wind strength from 5 kts to 18 kts:

A   Will change radiation fog to advection fog.

B   Will have no effect.

C   May cause the fog to lift and become low stratus.

8 Which of the following never appear in a TAF?

A   QNH

B   Temperature

C   Both A & B

9 The following shows:

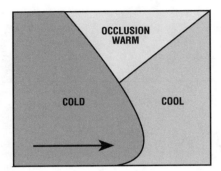

A A cold occlusion

B A cold front

C A warm occlusion

10 The conditions most suitable for the formation of radiation fog are:

A Cloudy night, moist air, small dewpoint spread.

B Cloudless night, dry cool air, moderate winds.

C Cloudless night, light winds, moist air.

11 Stability of the air is likely to be reduced when:

A There is cooling from below

B There is warming from below

C Water vapour is added to the air

12 When flying towards a depression at a constant indicated altitude, without updating the altimeter subscale setting, the aircraft's actual altitude will be:

A Lower than indicated

B Higher than indicated

C The same as indicated

13 Fill the missing words.
Radiation fog can thicken in the early morning when _____ mixing increases because of _____.

A Turbulence, Insolation

B Radiation, Conduction

C Turbulence, Advection

14 In the international standard atmosphere, mean sea level pressure is:

A 29.92 inches of mercury

B 1225 grams per cubic metre

C 14.7 grams per square inch

NOW REFER TO LAPFORM TEN

15 What is the 2000' wind at EGGD?

A 170/30 gusting 39kts

B 200/30

C 185/28

16 What is the surface temperature at 55N - 0730W

A 9.5°C

B 12.5°C

C 14°C

17 Zone 2 shows a:

A Warm occluded front

B A cold occluded front

C A quasi stationary front

18 You are planning a flight from Biggin Hill airfield (south of London) to Bembridge on the Isle of Wight. You are a PPL without an IMC or Instrument Rating and your flight is planned to take place entirely in 'the open FIR' - e.g. Class G airspace - below 3000' AMSL. You will be flying a PA 28 Warrior (IAS 105 knots) with one passenger. Your ETD is 1800 Z, with an en-route time of 55 minutes. Assuming you wish to complete the flight safely and legally, which of the following statements is true:

A There is no doubt that the flight can be safely and legally completed and you should depart on time.

B Assuming flight at an altitude to allow adequate terrain clearance, there is the probability that at times the cloud base will be at, or below, the operating altitude. Additionally a front is approaching the route and destination airfield. Cancel the flight.

C By delaying the flight two hours the front will clear the area and, daylight permitting, the flight can proceed.

19 The least visibility in zone 4 is?

A 20 mile deterioration to 8nm

B 20 km occasionally 8km

C 20 km isolated 8km

20 Lowest cloud forecast in zone 1?

A 1500'

B 200'

C 150'

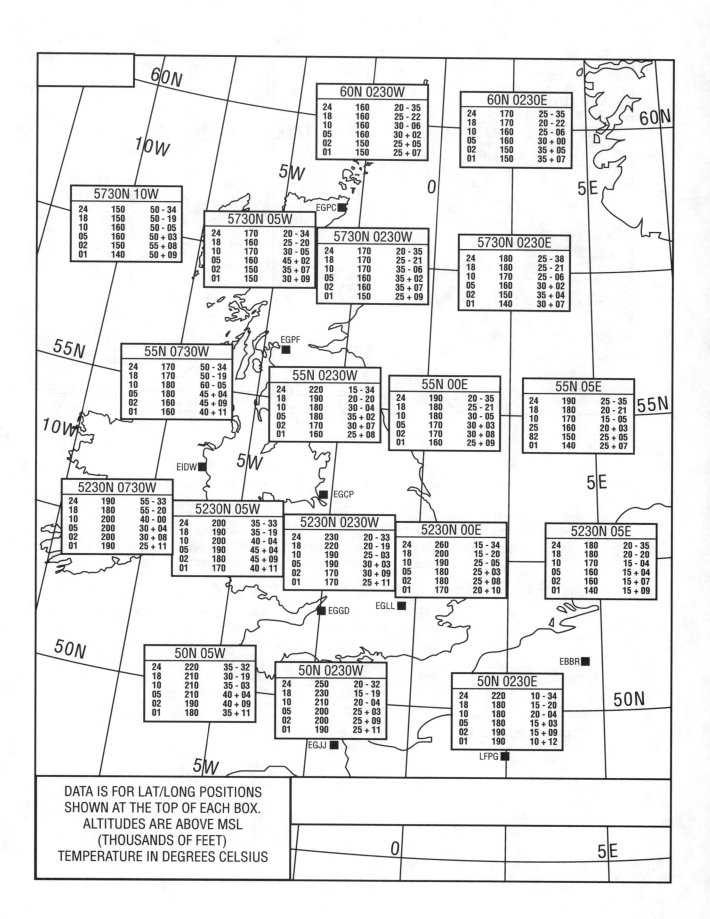

60N 0230W

24	160	20 - 35
18	160	25 - 22
10	160	30 - 06
05	160	30 + 02
02	150	25 + 05
01	150	25 + 07

60N 0230E

24	170	25 - 35
18	170	20 - 22
10	160	25 - 06
05	160	30 + 00
02	150	35 + 05
01	150	35 + 07

5730N 10W

24	150	50 - 34
18	150	50 - 19
10	160	50 - 05
05	160	50 + 03
02	150	55 + 08
01	140	50 + 09

5730N 05W

24	170	20 - 34
18	160	25 - 20
10	170	30 - 05
05	160	45 + 02
02	150	35 + 07
01	150	30 + 09

5730N 0230W

24	170	20 - 35
18	170	25 - 21
10	170	35 - 06
05	160	35 + 02
02	160	35 + 07
01	150	25 + 09

5730N 0230E

24	180	25 - 38
18	180	25 - 21
10	170	25 - 06
05	160	30 + 02
02	150	35 + 04
01	140	30 + 07

55N 0730W

24	170	50 - 34
18	170	50 - 19
10	180	60 - 05
05	180	45 + 04
02	160	45 + 09
01	160	40 + 11

55N 0230W

24	220	15 - 34
18	190	20 - 20
10	180	30 - 04
05	180	35 + 02
02	170	30 + 07
01	160	25 + 08

55N 00E

24	190	20 - 35
18	180	25 - 21
10	180	30 - 05
05	170	30 + 03
02	170	30 + 08
01	160	25 + 09

55N 05E

24	190	25 - 35
18	180	20 - 21
10	170	15 - 05
25	160	20 + 03
82	150	25 + 05
01	140	25 + 07

5230N 0730W

24	190	55 - 33
18	180	55 - 20
10	200	40 - 00
05	200	30 + 04
02	200	30 + 08
01	190	25 + 11

5230N 05W

24	200	35 - 33
18	190	35 - 19
10	200	40 - 04
05	190	45 + 04
02	180	45 + 09
01	170	40 + 11

5230N 0230W

24	230	20 - 33
18	220	20 - 19
10	190	25 - 03
05	190	30 + 03
02	170	30 + 09
01	170	25 + 11

5230N 00E

24	260	15 - 34
18	200	15 - 20
10	190	25 - 05
05	180	25 + 03
02	180	25 + 08
01	170	20 + 10

5230N 05E

24	180	20 - 35
18	180	20 - 20
10	170	15 - 04
05	160	15 + 04
02	160	15 + 07
01	140	15 + 09

50N 05W

24	220	35 - 32
18	210	30 - 19
10	210	35 - 03
05	210	40 + 04
02	190	40 + 09
01	180	35 + 11

50N 0230W

24	250	20 - 32
18	230	15 - 19
10	210	20 - 04
05	200	25 + 03
02	200	25 + 09
01	190	25 + 11

50N 0230E

24	220	10 - 34
18	180	15 - 20
10	180	20 - 04
05	180	15 + 03
02	190	15 + 09
01	190	10 + 12

EGPC · EGPF · EGCP · EIDW · EGGD · EGLL · EBBR · EGJJ · LFPG

DATA IS FOR LAT/LONG POSITIONS SHOWN AT THE TOP OF EACH BOX. ALTITUDES ARE ABOVE MSL (THOUSANDS OF FEET) TEMPERATURE IN DEGREES CELSIUS

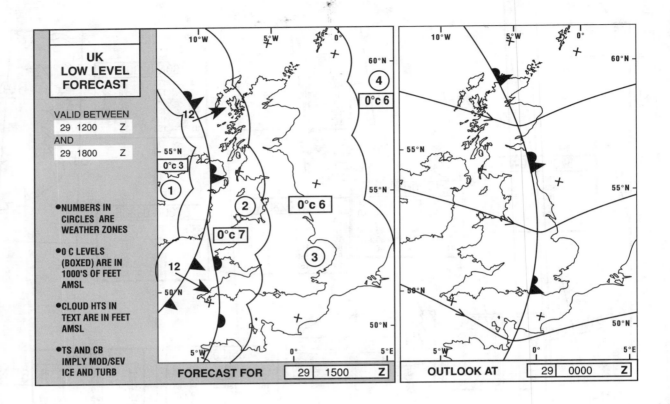

ZONE 1	GEN	30KM	NIL	6/8CUSC 2000/8000
	ONCL	8KM	RAIN SH	6/8CUSC 1500/12000
ZONE 2	GEN	14KM	NIL/RAIN	5/8SC 1500/6000 5/8LYR 8000/12000
	OCNL	8KM	RAIN	5/8ST 800/1500 8/8LYR 2000/17000
	ISOL FRONT	5000M	HEAVY RAIN	8/8LYR 500/20000
	ISOL	2000M	RAIN/DZ	8/8LYR 300/6000
ZONE 3	GEN	15KM	NIL	5/8CUSC 3000/6000
	OCNL	6KM	NIL	6/8STSC 1000/7000 6/8LYR 8000/10000
	ISOL	2500M	MIST/DZ	8/8STSC 500/7000
	ISOL SW	8KM	RAIN SH	6/8CUSC 2000/10000
ZONE 4	GEN	20KM	NIL	1/8SC 2500/6000
	ISOL	8KM	HAZE	1/8SC 2500/6000

OUTLOOK: UNTIL 29/0000Z:

Instructions

1   Time allowed 60 minutes.

2   Twenty multi-choice questions each carrying 5 marks. Marks are not deducted for wrong answers. The pass mark is 70%.

3   Read each question carefully as there is only one answer which is correct.

4   Remember examination technique, you are advised to pass over questions that seem difficult at first sight and return to them when you have answered the others.

5   Use the current edition of the relevant 1.500,000 ICAO chart.

Note:

Your navigation workings may not give you answers exactly as those given here, but they should be very close ie; within 2 degrees/knots and 1 mile/minute.

The safety altitudes have been calculated using the following technique.

The search area is a corridor 10nm each side of track, extending to a 10nm radius around the departure and arrival airfields. Within this area the highest fixed point is selected, which will be either the ground or a fixed structure.

In the case of the highest point being a structure, its altitude is rounded up to the next 100 feet, and then a 1000 foot safety margin is added, e.g. a mast 751ft AMSL gives a safety altitude of 1,800 feet (AMSL).

If the highest point is the ground, 299 feet is added to that figure to allow for a theoretical structure not required to be depicted on the chart (ie; less than 300 AGL). This figure is then rounded up to the nearest 100 feet and 1,000 feet safety margin is added to give the safety altitude e.g. if the highest point is a spot height 1426 ft AMSL. the safety altitude would be 2,800 feet (AMSL).

The above information is only given for information and guidance relevant to this publication. For operational procedures refer to your FTO (Flying Training Organisation).

1 What is the Rhumb Line track from Gloucestershire Airport (Staverton) (51° 53.5'N, 02° 10'W) to Peterborough (Sibson) Aerodrome? (52° 33'N, 00° 23'W)

A   055°

B   058°

C   245°

2 What is the distance from Gloucestershire Airport to Peterborough (Sibson) Aerodrome?

A   74 nm

B   80 nm

C   76 nm

3 TAS 100 kts, W/V 090° 20 kts, Track 010° (T) What is the Heading (T) and G/S?

A   019° 95 kts

B   022° 95 kts

C   022° 97 kts

4 Heading (T) 302°, Track 310°, G/S 120 kts, TAS 110 kts. What is the W/V?

A   188° 19 kts

B   182° 25 kts

C   182° 19 kts

5 An aircraft is flying from A to B, a distance of 130 nm at a G/S of 107 kts. After flying for 40 nm it is 7 nm to port of track. What alteration of heading is required to reach B?

A   15° port

B   17° starboard

C   15° starboard

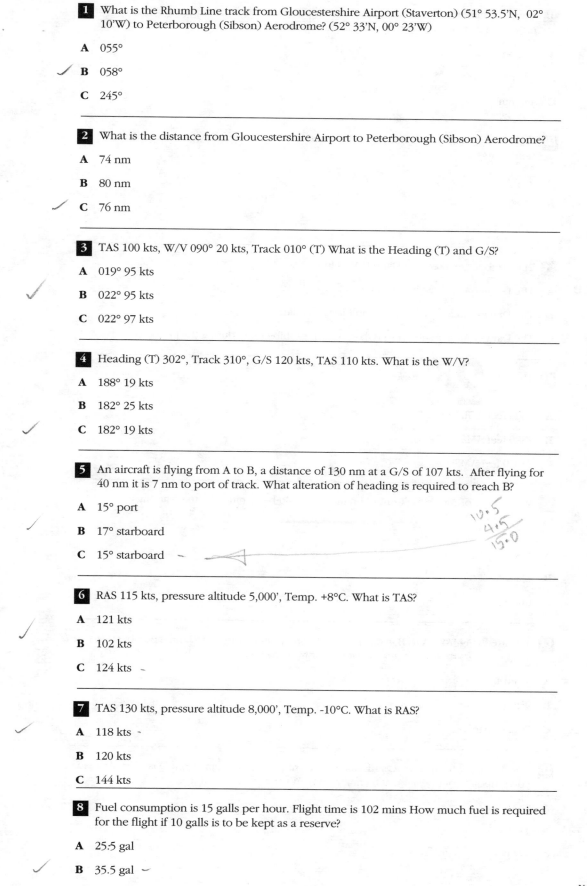

6 RAS 115 kts, pressure altitude 5,000', Temp. +8°C. What is TAS?

A   121 kts

B   102 kts

C   124 kts

7 TAS 130 kts, pressure altitude 8,000', Temp. -10°C. What is RAS?

A   118 kts

B   120 kts

C   144 kts

8 Fuel consumption is 15 galls per hour. Flight time is 102 mins How much fuel is required for the flight if 10 galls is to be kept as a reserve?

A   25:5 gal

B   35.5 gal

C   45.5 gal

9 Your fuel tank holds 40 gal and fuel consumption rate is 6.6 gal per hour. What is the maximum distance you can fly at a groundspeed of 70 kts?

A 430 nm

B 425 nm

C 432 nm

10 On a foreign map you notice ground marked at 830 m. How many feet does this represent?

A 2,730

B 2,780

C 2,700

11 The symbol * marked in a Danger Area indicates:

A The Danger Area is active at all times

B The Danger Area is active when notified by Notam

C The Danger Area is subject to Bylaws which prohibit entry during the period of activity

12 The MEF **2⁸** represents:

A 2800 feet AGL

B 2800 feet AMSL

C 28000 feet AMSL

13 Which type of Air Traffic Control boundary would be signified by the markings:

A MATZ

B Class A

C Class D

14 You are flying from A to B, a distance of 120 nm. After flying for 37 nm, you note that you are 3 nm to starboard of track. What is your track correction to reach B?

A 7° Port

B 9° Port

C 7° Starboard

15 You are flying from Q to R, a distance of 123 nm. Departure time from Q is 1203. At 1246 you pinpoint your position at 60 nm from Q. What is your ETA at R?

A 1335

B 1337

C 1331

16 In the UK, the magnetic compass will indicate a turn to the right when speed is decreased while heading:

A   West

B   East

C   South

---

17 In the UK, the turning errors in a magnetic compass are at a maximum when turning through headings of:

A   All headings

B   West and East

C   North and South

---

18 You are local flying around the Wash (53° 00'N 0° 20') and wish to penetrate the Marham MATZ. On what frequency should you make contact?

A   124.15

B   130.20

C   127.35

---

19 Within 5 nm of Shobdon (52° 14'N, 02° 53'W), what is the highest ground as indicated by Relief Portrayal?

A   500 - 1,000'

B   1,000 - 2,000'

C   2,000 - 3,000'

---

20 Decode the following symbol as found on ICAO charts:-

A   A mast rising to 1,700' amsl, 650' in height

B   A mast 1,700' high on ground 650'

C   A mast 650' high on ground 1,700' amsl

1 What is the true rhumb line track from A (52° 32'N, 0° 33'E) to B (52° 06'N, 02° 08'W) ?

A 255°

B 251°

C 075°

2 What is the distance from A to B?

A 100 nm

B 102 nm

C 106 nm

3 Given TAS 120 kts, W/V 060°/35 kts, Track 028°, what is the Heading (T)?

A 037°

B 033°

C 031°

4 Given TAS 120 kts, W/V 278°/ 30 kts, Track 217° (T), what is the G/S?

A 100 kts

B 108 kts

C 102 kts

5 Given Track 185° (T), Heading 197° (T), G/S 107 kts, and TAS 85 kts, what is the W/V?

A 330°/20 kts

B 315°/30 kts

C 328°/30 kts

6 Given TAS 120 kts, Heading 033° (T), Track 039°, G/S 150 kts, what is the W/V?

A 230°/32 kts

B 240°/22 kts

C 240°/32 kts

7 RAS 140 kts, pressure altitude 10,000', temperature +5°C, what is the TAS?

A 166 kts

B 169 kts

C 119 kts

8 Given pressure altitude 11,000', temp. -15°C, TAS 150 kts, what is the RAS?

A 132 kts

B 129 kts

C 175 kts

9 Your heading is 270° (T), G/S 115 kts, and distance of flight is 75 nm. After 30 nm you find that you are 5 nm to starboard of track. What is your new heading to reach your destination?

A 255°

B 253°

C 251°

10 You are flying from A to B, a distance of 95 nm, track 290°. After flying for 48 nm, you find that you are 4 nm to port of track. What is the required track to B from this point?

A 300°

B 303°

C 305°

11 An aircraft uses 19 gph flying at TAS 110 kts. How much fuel is required to make a flight of 230 nm, against a headwind of 15 kts, if a reserve of 18 galls is to be carried?

A 64 galls

B 62 galls

C 66 galls

12 Your fuel tank holds 26 galls, and your fuel consumption rate is 4.8 gph. What is the maximum distance you can fly at a groundspeed of 87 kts?

A 482 nm

B 475 nm

C 470 nm

13 The map symbol ⊕ VRP ASHBOURNE means:

A A Visual Reporting Point, notified in the UK AIP.

B A Venting under Reduced Pressure site.

C A Variable Routing Procedure, notified in the AGA section of the UK AIP.

14 A runway length is declared as 935 metres. What is that in feet?

A 3,090'

B 4,010'

C 3,070'

15 You are flying from B to C, a distance of 87 nm. Departure time from B was 0915. At 0943 you find your position is 20 nm from C. What is your ETA at C?

A 09:53

B 09:51

C 09:56

16 When accelerating on a Northerly heading in the UK, the magnetic compass will:

A   Show an apparent turn to the North

B   Show an apparent turn to the South

C   Show the same value of heading

17 On an ICAO chart, what does the following symbol mean?

A   Hang-Gliding

B   Microlight flying

C   Parachuting

18 Express 39.5 US gallons as litres:

A   150 l

B   180 l

C   160 l

19 The danger area at Lydd is marked D.044/3.2. Confirm that the Danger Area is active up to a level of:

A   3,200' amsl

B   3,200' agl

C   32,000'

20 On a flight from Rochester (51°21'N, 00°30'E) to Birmingham (52°27'N, 01°44'W), how many Altimeter Setting Regions will you fly in?

A   1

B   2

C   3

It is planned to carry out a VFR flight from Chichester/ Goodwood (50° 51'N 0° 46'W) to Shobdon (52° 14'N 2° 53'W) via Grove (51° 36'N 1° 27'W).

Complete the attached flight plan and answer questions 1 to 20 below.

1 What is the track (°T) from Goodwood to Grove?

A 325°(T)

B 330°(T)

C 327°(T)

2 What is the distance (nm) from Grove to Shobdon?

A 68nm

B 66nm

C 64.5nm

3 What is the estimated flight time from Goodwood to Shobdon?

A 103 mins

B 93 mins

C 90 mins

4 Using the flight plan time, a fuel consumption of 5 gallons/hour plus a reserve of 4 gallons overhead the destination, what is the minimum fuel required?

A 11.75 Gallons

B 11 Gallons

C 10.75 Gallons

5 Goodwood runway 10/28 is listed as being 613 metres long. What is that in feet?

A 2010ft

B 2000ft

C 1810ft

6 Goodwood Tower reports the surface wind as being 220/15. Your aircraft has a crosswind limit of 12 knots and you may not accept a tailwind component. Runways 06/24; 10/28 and 14/32 are available. Which runways are within your aircraft's limits?

A 24

B 10/28

C 14/32

You get airborne at 1300 UTC and set heading overhead Goodwood at 1305 UTC.

7 At 1332 you pinpoint your position as 2nm east of 51° 18' N 1° 14' W. Using the groundspeed experienced from overhead Goodwood, what is the revised ETA for Grove?

A 1345

B 1349

C 1352

8 What is the height of the mast at position 51° 34' N 1° 31' W above sea level?

A 856ft

B 233ft

C 993ft ~ 1013 .

9 What station would you call and on what frequency to obtain a Lower Airspace Radar Service in the vicinity of Basingstoke?

A 109.6

B 125.25

C 126.7

10 Approaching Grove, in order to avoid traffic, you turn onto a compass heading of 270°. Compass deviation is 3° E. What is your True Heading? Take variation as 5°W.

A 267°

B 268°

C 272°

11 Overhead Grove, Air Traffic asks you to turn onto a westerly heading. Unfortunately your DI has failed. Onto what heading should you roll out using the magnetic compass?

A 272°

B 268°

C 270°

12 You are overhead Grove at 1345 UTC and your remaining fuel is 12 gallons. Assuming flight plan time from here to Shobdon, with a consumption of 5 gallons/hour, what will be your remaining endurance at Shobdon?

A 1hr 30 mins

B 1hr 20 mins

C 1hr 40 mins

13 Just after setting heading at Grove for Shobdon, you ask Brize Radar for the Regional Pressure Settings for the rest of your flight. What Region(s) do you require?

A Portland

B Chatham

C Cotswold & Barnsley

14 On the leg from Grove to Shobdon, having held your planned heading, you pinpoint your position as overhead Windrush (51° 48' N 1° 44' W). Assuming no further change of wind velocity, what heading alteration is needed to fly to Shobdon?

A 12° Port

B 12° Starboard

C 15° Port

15 Later on, you find yourself 3 nm due east of Ledbury (52° 02' N 2° 36' W). What aerial activity might you expect to see there?

A   Parachuting

B   Hang-Gliding

C   Microlight Flying

16 Given a RAS of 85 knots, pressure altitude 3500 feet, OAT +2°C, what is the TAS?

A   90kts

B   83kts

C   88kts

17 Given heading 295°(True), Track 306°(True), TAS 85 knots, G/S 72 knots, find the W/V.

A   250°/20kts

B   240°/18kts

C   245°/15kts

18 In order to ensure a clearance of 1,000 feet above any high ground/obstacle within 10 nm of planned track, what is the minimum altitude at which the whole flight can be made (rounded up to the nearest 100 feet)?

A   2800ft

B   2500ft

C   2600ft

19 What does the symbol 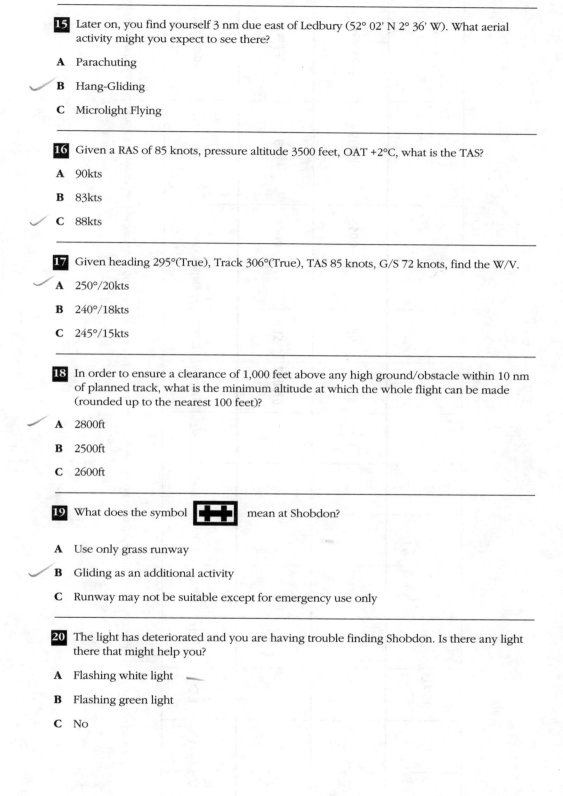 mean at Shobdon?

A   Use only grass runway

B   Gliding as an additional activity

C   Runway may not be suitable except for emergency use only

20 The light has deteriorated and you are having trouble finding Shobdon. Is there any light there that might help you?

A   Flashing white light

B   Flashing green light

C   No

Latitude and longitude are given as an aid to identification but where locations and facilities are marked on the chart, their charted positions should be used.

From	To	FL/Alt	Safety Alt ft amsl	Tas kt	W/V	Trk T	Drift	Hdg T	Var	Hdg M	GS kt	Dist nm	Time hr/min
Goodwood	Grove	3000		85	250/20	320		316	+	320	80	52	34m
Goodwood	Shobdon	3500		85	270/15	306					73	66	54
										Total			

You are to plan a VFR cross country from Shoreham (50°50'N) (00°01.7'W) to Stapleford (51°39'N) (00°00.9'E) via Canterbury (51°17.5'N) (01°00'E).

Complete the attached flight plan and answer questions 1 to 20 below

---

1 What is your Track ('T') from Shoreham to Canterbury?

A   061°(T)

B   064°(T)

C   058°(T)

---

2 What is the distance (nm) from Shoreham to Canterbury?

A   58nm

B   55nm

C   56nm

---

3 What is the estimated flight time from Shoreham to Canterbury?

A   35mins

B   40mins

C   37mins

---

4 Using the total flight plan time, an average fuel consumption of 22 litres per hour, plus a reserve of 22 litres overhead the destination, what is the minimum fuel required in IMP gallons?

A   9.9 gallons

B   9.5 gallons

C   9.2 gallons

---

5 Shoreham's runway 03/21 is 824 metres, what is that in feet?

A   2750ft

B   2700ft

C   2650ft

---

6 Shoreham tower reports the surface wind as being 140/15. Your aircraft has a crosswind limit of 12 knots, and you may not accept a tailwind component. Runways 03/21; 07/25; 13/31 are available. Which runway is within your aircraft's limits?

A   13

B   03

C   25

You are airborne at 1100 utc and set heading overhead Shoreham at 1105 UTC.

7 At 1123 utc you pinpoint your position as 1 nm east of (N5104) (E00020). Using the groundspeed experienced from overhead Shoreham, what is the revised ETA for Canterbury

A   1140.5 UTC

B   1143 UTC

C   1138.5 UTC

8 What is the level of the ground (AMSL), where a mast is located at (N5117.5) (E0059)?

A   300ft

B   381ft

C   336ft

9 What frequency would you select to contact Southend?

A   124.60

B   129.45

C   128.95

10 Halfway along track from Canterbury to Stapleford, located at (51°24'N) (00°36'E) there is a red circle with M in the centre. What does this mean?

A   Marshes

B   Area of intense microlight activity

C   Minefield

11 Approaching Southend just south of Minster, in order to avoid traffic, you are asked to turn onto a compass heading of 270°. Compass deviation is 6°E. What is your true heading?

A   268°

B   272°

C   276°

12 Just south of St. Marys Marsh VRP you have 24 litres of fuel on board. How much will you have left on board in terms of endurance when you arrive overhead Stapleford. Assume fuel consumption of 22 litres per hour.

A   52 mins

B   50 mins

C   55 mins

13 At Thurrock, to what altitude does the LTMA descend?

A   3500ft

B   2499ft

C   2500ft

14 What is located on the airfield at Stapleford (Refer to legend)

A Microlight Activity

B Customs (24hrs)

✓ C Lambourne VOR

15 Stapleford's runways are 22/04 and 10/28. The reported surface wind is 160/12. What runway would be most suitable to use, bearing in mind a crosswind limit of 12 kts and no tailwind component allowed?

A 04

✓ B 10

C Both A & B

16 What would be the crosswind component if you use runway 10?

A 13 kts

B 9 kts

✓ C 10 kts

17 What site is located just outside Stapleford's ATZ to the south west?

A Parachuting

B Parascending

C Hang-Gliding

18 In order to ensure a clearance of 1000ft above any high ground/obstacle within 10 nm of planned track, what is the minimum altitude at which the whole flight can be made (rounded up to the nearest 100ft).

✓ A 2100ft

B 2000ft

C 1800ft

19 Given a RAS of 85 kts, an altitude of 4500ft and an OAT of -3°C, what is the TAS?

✓ A 89 kts

B 81 kts

C 83 kts

20 Given a heading of 180°(T), track 168°(T), TAS 85 kts G/S 96kts, find the W/V

A 120/22

B 235/22

✓ C 295/22

Latitude and longitude are given as an aid to identification but where locations and facilities are marked on the chart, their charted positions should be used.

From	To	FL/Alt	Safety Alt ft amsl	Tas kt	W/V	Trk T	Drift	Hdg T	Var	Hdg M	GS kt	Dist nm	Time hr/min
Shoreham	Canterbury	2,000		85	175/15	060		070	3·5	074/073	90	56	38 (37.5)
Canterbury	Stapleford	2,000		85	190/20	305		298	3·5	301/302	94/95	38	24
											Total		

It is planned to carry out a VFR cross-country from Hucknall (53°00'N) (01°13'W) to Manchester Airport (53°21N) (02°16'W) via a turning point at Hawarden (53°10'N) (02°58'W). Please complete the attached flight log before answering the questions.

1 What is the distance in nm from Hucknall to Hawarden?

A   64 nm

B   62 nm

C   63.5 nm

2 What amount of drift is being experienced on the first leg?

A   3° Port

B   4° Starboard

C   3° Starboard

3 If the average fuel consumption is estimated to be 25 litres/hour and you are required to have 45mins reserves and 30mins diversion fuel; how much fuel (U S Gals) are you required to start with?

A   13 gals

B   16 gals

C   15 gals

4 What is the track (T) from Hucknall to Hawarden

A   277°

B   279°

C   281°

5 Hucknall's level above mean sea level is:

A   459ft

B   515ft

C   281ft

You are airborne at 1115 UTC and find yourself overhead Congleton VRP 53°10'N 02°13'W at 1150 UTC

6 At 1150 UTC what do you estimate the W/V to be?

A   075/24

B   305/24

C   255/24

7 You note that you are now in the Manchester CTA. Whom would you contact to explain?

A   Manchester radar 119.4

B   Manchester ATC 119.85

C   Daventry control 119.65

8 Using the revised position and W/V, what is the new heading (°M) and ETA direct for Hawarden?

A   261° 1209 UTC

B   271° 1218 UTC

C   261° 1215 UTC

9 The restricted area (53°16' N 02°57'W) just north of Hawarden extends to what level?

A   31,000ft AMSL

B   2200ft AGL

C   2200ft AMSL

10 Your airborne time from Hawarden to Manchester is?

A   17 mins

B   15 mins

C   14 mins

11 What is the track (T) from Manchester to Hawarden?

A   247°

B   067°

C   065°

12 Are you allowed to fly through an active danger area?

A   Never

B   Sometimes when local bylaws permit

C   Yes always if you are in two way communication with a danger area crossing service (DACS)

13 Half way between Hawarden and Manchester, ATC ask you to steer a compass heading of 030°. If deviation is 2°E and local magnetic variation is taken to be 6°W, what is your true heading?

A   026°

B   035°

C   021°

14 Using the revised flight time from Hucknall to Hawarden and the planned flight time from Hawarden to Manchester, how much fuel will you have left on board from the amount required in Question 3?

A   20 ltrs

B   35 ltrs

C   28 ltrs

15 The Manchester CTR extends from:

A SFC - 3500 ALT

B 3500 ALT - FL 245

C 2500 ALT - 3500 ALT

You are enroute from A to B, a distance of 85nm. After 35nm you are 5nm off track.

16 What heading change must you make to regain track 35nm further on?

A 8°

B 17°

C 15°

17 What heading change must you make to regain track overhead destination (B) to the nearest whole degree.

A 13°

B 15°

C 16°

18 Select the correct answer for the following missing information:

TR(T)	W/V	HDG(T)	VAR	HDG(M)	DEV	HDG(C)	RAS	ALT TEMP	TAS	G/S	DIST	TIME
149	290/30	?	7W	?	4E	?	110kt	8000 -10	?	?	?	25

A 158, 151, 155, 122, 145, 60

B 158, 165, 161, 130, 156, 65

C 158, 165, 161, 122, 145, 60

19 An aircraft is descending from a flight level to an altitude, toward an airfield to land. Assuming no further flight level reports have been requested, what altimeter setting should be used ?

A Regional QNH

B Aerodrome QNH

C Aerodrome QFE

20 A blue solid triangle ▲ means:

A An on-request reporting point

B A compulsory reporting point

C Special access lane entry/exit

Latitude and longitude are given as an aid to identification but where locations and facilities are marked on the chart, their charted positions should be used.

From	To	FL/Alt	Safety Alt ft amsl	Tas kt	W/V	Trk T	Drift	Hdg T	Var	Hdg M	GS kt	Dist nm	Time hr/min
Hucknall (53°00'N) (01°13'W)	Hawarden	3,000		85	260/15	280		276	5W	281	70	64	55 min
Hawarden	Manchester (53°21'N) (02°16'W)	2,000		90	280/20	066		058	5W	063	100	28	17.
										Total		92	112

NAV 22

It is planned to carry out a VFR cross-country from Skegness (53° 11'N) (00° 20'E) to Netherthorpe (53° 19'N) (01° 11'W) via a turning point at Hucknall (53° 00'N) (01° 13'W).
Please complete the attached flight log before answering the following questions.

---

1 What is the distance from Skegness to Hucknall in km?

A 106 km

B 92 km

C 57 km

---

2 What amount of drift are you experiencing on the first leg?

A 10° Port

B 13° Starboard

C 13° Port

---

3 What is your magnetic track from Skegness to Hucknall?

A 265°

B 277°

C 259°

---

4 What is the estimated flight time from Skegness to Hucknall?

A 41 mins

B 38.5 mins

C 35 mins

---

5 What is your groundspeed from Hucknall to Netherthorpe?

A 66 kts

B 129 kmh

C 84 mph

---

6 Using the highest possible fixed object within 10nm of track plus 1000ft for the safety altitude, what is the safety altitude to the nearest 100ft from Skegness to Hucknall?

A 1600ft AMSL

B 1800ft AMSL

C 1900ft AMSL

---

7 Assuming the average fuel consumption for the flight is 4.7 IMP gallons per hour and you require 45 mins reserves and 30 mins diversion fuel, what is the total fuel (in US gallons) required for the flight?

A 15.3 US gallons

B 12.1 US gallons

C 10.1 US gallons

8 What is the distance from Hucknall to Netherthorpe to the nearest half nautical mile?

A   17 nm

B   18.5 nm

C   20 nm

9 What is your heading (°T) from Hucknall to Netherthorpe?

A   001°

B   003°

C   358°

10 What is the altitude of Netherthorpe above sea level?

A   250ft AMSL

B   310ft AMSL

C   515ft AMSL

11 D305/1.5 (53°05'N) (00°11'W) is a:

A   Scheduled danger area active during published hours

B   Notified danger area inactive unless notified by class 1 notam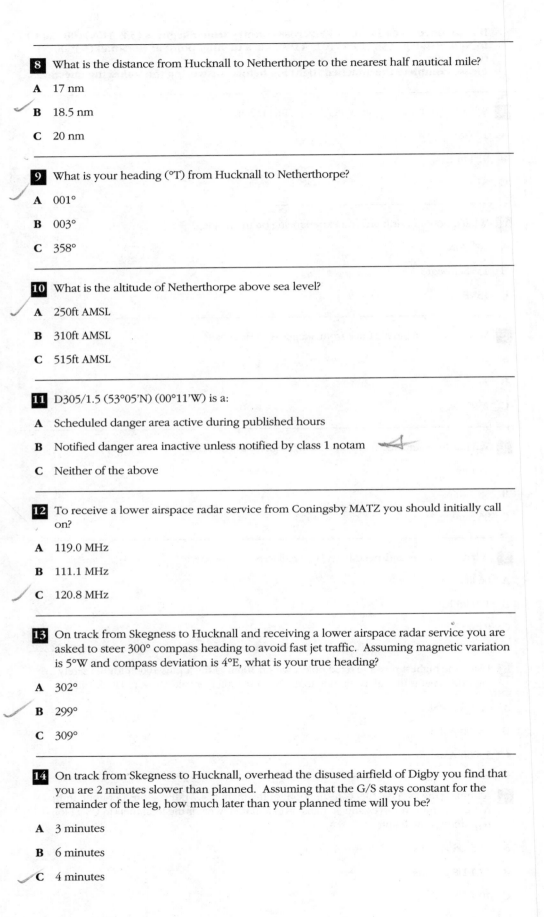

C   Neither of the above

12 To receive a lower airspace radar service from Coningsby MATZ you should initially call on?

A   119.0 MHz

B   111.1 MHz

C   120.8 MHz

13 On track from Skegness to Hucknall and receiving a lower airspace radar service you are asked to steer 300° compass heading to avoid fast jet traffic. Assuming magnetic variation is 5°W and compass deviation is 4°E, what is your true heading?

A   302°

B   299°

C   309°

14 On track from Skegness to Hucknall, overhead the disused airfield of Digby you find that you are 2 minutes slower than planned. Assuming that the G/S stays constant for the remainder of the leg, how much later than your planned time will you be?

A   3 minutes

B   6 minutes

C   4 minutes

15 Approximately five NM to the west of Netherthorpe is Rother Valley. What primary activity takes place there?

A Cable launched parascending parachute site.

B Parachuting.

C Microlight and kite flying activity.

16 At your turning point at Hucknall the wind increases in strength to 25kts at your planned level. Assuming you were airborne from Skegness at 0850 UTC, and your planned time for the first leg was correct, what is your revised estimate for Netherthorpe?

A 0941 UTC

B 0950 UTC

C 0946 UTC

17 An MEF **3²** represents:

A Maximum Elevation Figure - this is NOT a safety altitude.

B Minimum Elevation for Flight

C Maximum Elevation Figure - the approved safety height in that area.

18 If an aircraft has a true track of 287° a true airspeed of 94 kts, a true heading of 272° and a groundspeed of 94 kts, what is the wind velocity?

A 010/25kts

B 180/20kts

C 190/25kts

19 Convert 258lbs of AVGAS at a specific gravity of 0.72 to US gallons.

A 36 US gallons

B 43 US gallons

C 95 US gallons

20 With a RAS of 95kts a pressure altitude of 7000ft and an outside temperature of -5°C, what is your TAS?

A 104kts

B 93kts

C 87kts

Latitude and longitude are given as an aid to identification but where locations and facilities are marked on the chart, their charted positions should be used.

From	To	FL/Alt Safety Alt ft amsl	Tas kt	W/V	Trk T	Drift	Hdg T	Var	Hdg M	GS kt	Dist nm	Time hr/min
Skegness (53°11'N) (00°20'E)	**Hucknall** (53°00'N) (01°13'W)	2,000		85	010/20	261	13	274	5W	279	89	57	32/39 nm
Hucknall	**Netherthorpe** (53°19'N) (01°11'W)	2,000		85	350/15	003		000	5W	005	70	18	15
	Total										(69)		

You are to plan a VFR cross-country from Bournemouth (50°46'N) (01°50'W) to Dunkeswell (50°51'N) (03°13'W) then to Bristol (51°22'N) (02°42'W). Complete the attached flight plan and answer questions 1 to 15 below:

1 What is your track (T°) from Bournemouth to Dunkeswell?

A   270°

B   275°

C   273°

2 What is your magnetic heading from Bournemouth to Dunkeswell?

A   270°

B   275°

C   265°

3 What is the estimated flight time from Bournemouth to Dunkeswell?

A   50 mins

B   41.5 mins

C   40 mins

4 Using the planned flight time from Bournemouth to Dunkeswell and assuming a fuel consumption of approximately 5 imp gallons per hour, plus a required reserve of 6 imp gallons overhead Dunkeswell, what is the required fuel in litres for that leg?

A   40 litres

B   43 litres

C   39 litres

5 Bournemouth's 26/08 runway is 1838m. What is that in feet?

A   6100ft

B   6090ft

C   6028ft

6 Bournemouth tower reports the surface wind as 190/12. Your aircraft has a crosswind limit of 10kts and you may not accept a tailwind component. Runways 08/26 and 17/35 are available, which runway would you choose to use?

A   17

B   26

C   35

You are airborne at 0930 UTC and set heading overhead Bournemouth at 0935 UTC.

7 At 0955 you pinpoint your position as being 2nm north of Beaminster (50°49'N) (02°45'W). Using the revised groundspeed, what is the new ETA for Dunkeswell?

A 1006 UTC

B 1014 UTC

C 1009 UTC

8 What is the elevation of Dunkeswell?

A 915ft AMSL

B 850ft AMSL

C 921ft AMSL

9 What feature is most visible at (50°48'N) (02°29'W)?

A chalk giant

B white chalk horse

C woodland

10 On track from Dunkeswell to Bristol, just south of Taunton on the M5 there is an 'S' in a red circle. What does this mean?

A Motorway service area

B Special police area

C Subterranean cables

11 Approaching Bridgewater, Yeovilton radar ask you to steer a compass heading of north to avoid low level jet traffic. If compass deviation is assumed to be 3°E and the local magnetic variation 5°W, what is your true heading?

A 358°

B 355°

C 357°

12 Overhead Cannington (51°09'N) (03°04'W) you are asked to resume your own navigation. What is your magnetic heading to Bristol?

A 043°

B 034°

C 041°

13 Assuming you maintain your desired track, from what altitude does the Bristol CTA commence?

A 1500ft

B 6500ft

C SFC

14 What frequency would you use to contact Bristol for homing information?

A 125.85

B 127.35

C 132.4

15 What does ⎡ **BRISTOL** ⎤ mean outlined in magenta?

A Runway length greater than 1850m

B Customs facilities available

C Operated subject to certain times

16 Given a RAS of 114 kts, a pressure altitude of 6000' and a temperature of 0°C. What is the TAS?

A 125kts

B 124kts

C 123kts

17 Given a heading of 151°(T), track of 157°(T), TAS of 98kts, G/S of 114kts, find the W/V.

A 010°/20kts

B 020°/20kts

C 015°/15kts

18 What does the following magenta symbol mean:

A Bird sanctuary

B High intensity radio transmission area

C Gas venting station

19 You are en-route in a straight line from one aerodrome to another. You notice that after 15nm you are 2nm off track. Assuming you have another 20nm to go, by how much will you alter heading to arrive overhead at destination. Use the 1 in 60 rule.

A 12°

B 8°

C 14°

20 When turning through south in the UK and using the magnetic compass the pilot should:

A Undershoot the desired heading.

B Overshoot the desired heading.

C Stop the turn immediately the compass indicates the desired heading.

Latitude and longitude are given as an aid to identification but where locations and facilities are marked on the chart, their charted positions should be used.

From	To	FL/Alt	Safety Alt ft amsl	Tas kt	W/V	Trk T	Drift	Hdg T	Var	Hdg M	GS kt	Dist nm	Time hr/min
Bournemouth (50°46'N) (01°50'W)	Dunkeswell (50°51'N) (03°13'W)	2,000		90	220/20	276	10R	266	5W	271	77	53	41.5
Dunkeswell	Bristol (51°25'N) (02°42'W)	1,500		95	260/25	032	2R	030	5W	035	114	37	19.5
										Total		90	61

It is planned to carry out a VFR cross-country from Gloucester Staverton airport (51°53'N) (02°10'W) to Cambridge (52°12'N) (00°11'E) via Northampton Sywell (52°18'N) (00°48'W). Please complete the attached flight log and then answer the questions

---

1 What is the true heading from Staverton to Northampton?

A 073°

B 076°

C 079°

---

2 What is your estimated groundspeed from Staverton to Northampton?

A 103kts

B 105kts

C 100kts

---

3 What amount of drift are you experiencing on the first leg?

A 10P

B 10S

C 12P

---

4 On the first leg what is the safety altitude (FT AMSL) rounded up to the nearest hundred feet. Use the highest fixed object within 10nm of track.

A 2000ft

B 2100ft

C 2200ft

---

5 What is your estimated enroute airborne time on the first leg?

A 30 mins

B 32.5 mins

C 36 mins

---

6 What altimeter setting regions do you enter, on the entire route, in order?

A Chatham, Barnsley, Cotswold

B Barnsley, Chatham, Cotswold

C Cotswold, Barnsley, Chatham

---

7 You wish to descend from 9000' to 2000' in 5 minutes, the required Rate of Descent is :

A 900 feet/minute

B 1200 feet/minute

C 1400 feet/minute

8 What height is the mast above ground level, located at (52°12'N) (01°15'W)?

A 1112ft

B 388ft

C 325ft

9 Assuming an average fuel consumption of 5 US gallons per hour with 45 mins reserves and 30 mins diversion fuel required, using the planned route time, how much fuel in litres is required?

A 42 litres

B 44.2 litres

C 40 litres

10 On the first leg, after 21nm, you realise that you are 6nm off track to the north, how much and in what direction would you alter heading to regain track at Northampton?

A 17° right

B 27° right

C 20° left

11 What is your magnetic track from Northampton to Cambridge?

A 099°

B 110°

C 104°

12 What is the distance in statute miles from Northampton to Cambridge?

A 66.5

B 36

C 41.5

13 What is Northampton's altitude above mean sea level?

A 131m

B 378.5ft

C 429m

14 Assuming you were airborne from Gloucester at 1414UTC and flight log time was correct for the first leg, what is your ETA for Cambridge if the wind on the second leg was 170/15?

A 1514 UTC

B 1515 UTC

C 1512 UTC

15 On the second leg, what is the contact frequency for the Bedford MATZ?

A   391.5

B   124.4   NO   MATZ !!

C   293

16 An aircraft has a Maximum Take Off Weight (MTOW) of 2440 lbs/1106 Kg. The aircraft loading (without fuel) is:

Basic Aircraft 1515 lbs

Pilot and passengers 600 lbs

Baggage 37 lbs

Ignoring balance and performance considerations, what is the maximum fuel (in US gals) that can be carried without exceeding the MTOW, assuming a Sp G of 0.72 ?

A   40 US gal

B   46 US gal

C   48 US gal

17 What does the small magenta circle at position (53°16.5'N)(00°15'W) represent?

A   Gas venting site up to 3500ft AMSL

B   Gun velocity site active up to 3200ft AMSL

C   Ground visual station 3.2nm diameter

18 Select the correct answer that completes the following table:

TR(T)	W/V	HDG(T)	VAR	HDG(M)	DEV	HDG(C)	RAS	ALT TEMP	TAS	G/S	DIST	TIME
192	?	188	6W	?	?	192	?	4000 -10	108	121	85	?

A   030/12, 182, 10E, 110, 42

B   042/25, 192, 0, 100, 43

C   042/15, 194, 2E, 105, 42

19 The figure **0⁹** to the north of Cambridge represents:

A   The minimum safety altitude for that area.

B   The height (AGL) of the highest man-made obstruction in that area.

C   The maximum elevation of known and possible unmarked features in that area.

20 By the size of Cambridge's ATZ, what must the runway length be greater than?

A   1850m

B   1800m

C   1750m

Latitude and longitude are given as an aid to identification but where locations and facilities are marked on the chart, their charted positions should be used.

From	To	FL/Alt	Safety Alt ft amsl	Tas kt	W/V	Trk T	Drift	Hdg T	Var	Hdg M	GS kt	Dist nm	Time hr/min
Gloucester Staverton (51°23'N) (02°10'W)	Northampton Sywell (52°18'N) (00°48'W)	3,000		92	190/22	064	11L	075	5W	080	103	56	33
Northampton Sywell	Cambridge (52°12'N) (00°11'E)	2,000		90	180/18	099	12L (9L)	111 (108)	5W	116 (113)	85 (83)	36	25.5 (26)
											Total		

It is planned to carry out a VFR cross-country from Bembridge, Isle of Wight (50°41'N) (01°06'W) to Blackbushe (51°20'N) (00°50'W) via a turning point at Thruxton (51°13'N) (01°36'W). Please complete the attached flight log before answering the questions.

1 What is your true track from Bembridge to Thruxton?

A 327°

B 330°

C 333°

2 What drift is the aircraft experiencing on the first leg?

A 10° Starboard

B 10° Port

C 12° Starboard

3 What is your magnetic heading on the first leg?

A 323°

B 341°

C 248°

4 What is the distance in metres from Bembridge to Thruxton?

A 6850m

B 685000m

C 68500m

5 What is your estimated enroute time from Bembridge to Thruxton?

A 31 mins

B 30.5 mins

C 29.5 mins

6 Assuming a fuel consumption on the first leg of 6.1 US gallons per hour, how much fuel in total is used in pounds, using a specific gravity of 0.81 and the planned enroute time?

A 41 lbs

B 65.5 lbs

C 24.2 lbs

7 Initial contact to Southampton would be made on what frequency?

A 120.225

B 113.35

C 391.5

---

8 What is the safety altitude on the first leg rounded up to the nearest 100ft if the calculation is made by the highest fixed object within 10nm of track assuming 1000 ft clearance?

A 2200ft

B 2100ft

C 2400ft

---

9 What is the vertical extent of the Southampton CTR?

A 3000ft AMSL to FL55

B 1500ft AMSL to FL55

C Surface to 2000ft AMSL

---

10 What frequency would you initially call for a MATZ penetration on the first leg?

A 126.7

B 108.2

C 376

---

11 What is your magnetic track from Thruxton to Blackbushe?

A 076°

B 071°

C 081°

---

12 What is your estimated groundspeed on the second leg?

A 100kts

B 97kts

C 104kts

---

13 What is the distance from Thruxton to Blackbushe in feet?

A 17.630ft

B 176,320ft

C 1,763,200ft

---

14 Assuming you were airborne at 1610UTC and the flight log time was correct on the first leg, but the wind on the second leg was actually 285/12kts, what would be your revised ETA for Blackbushe?

A 1658 UTC

B 1706 UTC

C 1656 UTC

15 You wish to descend from 8500' to 2500' over a distance of 19 nautical miles, at a ground speed of 135 knots. What rate of descent is required ?

A 850 feet/min

B 610 feet/min

✓ **C** 710 feet/min

16 What ASR do you cross into on the second leg?

A Cotswold

B Portland

✓ **C** Chatham

17 Given a RAS of 98kts and a pressure altitude of 8000ft with an outside air temperature of +3°c, what is the TAS?

A 86kts

✓ **B** 111kts

C 113kts

18 If after 53nm you are off track by 6nm, what is the track error?

A 6°

✓ **B** 7°

C 8°

19 On the second leg, you are asked by Farnborough radar to steer a compass heading of 060° to avoid helicopter traffic. If deviation is 2E, what is your true heading?

A 067°

B 063°

✓ **C** 057°

20 Given a heading (T) of 050°, a groundspeed of 129kts a track (T) of 064° and a true airspeed of 142kts, calculate the wind velocity.

✓ **A** 348°/35kts

B 125°/35kts

C 300°/35kts

Latitude and longitude are given as an aid to identification but where locations and facilities are marked on the chart, their charted positions should be used.

From	To	FL/Alt Safety Alt ft amsl	Tas kt	W/V	Trk T	Drift	Hdg T	Var	Hdg M	GS kt	Dist nm	Time hr/min
Bembridge I.O.W. (50°41'N) (01°06'W)	Thruxton (51°13'N) (01°36'W)	3,000ft	85	270/18	330	11 R	319	5W	324	75	37	29.5
Thruxton	Blackbushe (51°20'N) (00°50'W)	2,500ft	82	290/22	076	3R (4L)	073 072	5W	078 075	99 (92)	29	17·5 (18)
										Total		

It is planned to carry out a VFR cross-country from Newcastle (55°02'N) (01°41'N) to Barrow (Walney Island) (54°08'N) (03°16'W) via a turning point at Carlisle (54°56'N) (02°48'W). Please complete the attached flight log before answering the questions.

1 What is the true track from Newcastle to Carlisle?

A 260°

B 261°

C 264°

2 What drift is being experienced on the first leg?

A 5°S

B 6°P

C 8°S

3 What is the magnetic heading on the first leg?

A 268°

B 261°

C 256°

4 What is the groundspeed on the first leg?

A 72kts

B 79sm/hr

C 69km/h

5 What is the airborne enroute time of the entire journey?

A 1hr 12mins

B 1hr 10mins

C 1hr 14mins

6 Assuming an average fuel consumption of 13.7kg per hour and a specific gravity of 0.72, how much fuel is used in imperial gallons?

A 5.14 IMP gallons

B 42 IMP gallons

C 24 IMP gallons

7 Using 1000ft above the highest fixed object within 10nm of track, what is the safety altitude on the first leg, rounded up to the nearest 100ft?

A 2800ft

B 3000ft

C 3500ft

8 On what frequency would you contact Newcastle approach?

A   126.35

B   118.5

C   114.25

9 What altimeter setting region are you in, when you leave   Newcastle?

A   Holyhead

B   Tyne

C   Barnsley

10 Approaching Carlisle you make use of the VDF facility and request a 'QDM'. This is:

A   A true heading to the facility in nil wind conditions

B   A true heading from the facility in nil wind conditions

C   A magnetic heading to the facility in nil wind conditions

11 What is the magnetic track from Carlisle to Barrow?

A   208°

B   205°

C   202°

12 What is the true heading on the second leg?

A   209°

B   198°

C   202°

13 What is the distance in KM from Carlisle to Barrow?

A   85km

B   51km

C   95km

14 what is the estimated airborne enroute time on the second leg?

A   38 mins

B   42 mins

C   40 mins

15 An aircraft has a Maximum Take Off Weight (MTOW) of 726Kg/1600lbs. It has a maximum useable fuel capacity of 85 litres. Ignoring balance and performance considerations, can the aircraft as loaded below carry full fuel and remain below the MTOW?

Basic Aircraft 525 kg

Pilot & Passenger 140 kg

Baggage 10 kg

Assume a SpG of 0.72

A Yes

B No

C Maybe - if authorised by the aircraft operator for aircraft with a public transport category C of A.

16 Given a TAS of 120 kts HDG 095° ground speed 95 kts track 085°, what is the W/V?

A 308/32

B 128/32

C 064/32

17 Approaching Barrow, the Manchester RASA extends:

A From FL55 to FL155 on 133.05

B From FL55 to FL150 on 124.45

C From SFC to FL150

18 What is the height of the MAST (AGL) at position (54°32'N) (03°36'W)?

A 350 ft

B 412 ft

C 622 ft

19 Assuming you were airborne from Newcastle at 1159UTC, the first leg time was correct, but on the second leg the W/V was 235/26, at what time do you arrive at Barrow?

A 1325 UTC

B 1311 UTC

C 1318 UTC

20 Choose the answer that correctly fills the missing spaces:

TR(T)	W/V	HDG(T)	VAR	HDG(M)	DEV	HDG(C)	RAS	ALT TEMP	TAS	G/S	DIST	TIME
159	290/30	?	7W	?	4E	?	105kt	8000 -10	?	?	?	25

A 155, 162, 161, 128, 150, 60

B 170, 117, 173, 116, 133, 55

C 160, 167, 163, 124, 148, 63

Latitude and longitude are given as an aid to identification but where locations and facilities are marked on the chart, their charted positions should be used.

From	To	FL/Alt	Safety Alt ft amsl	Tas kt	W/V	Trk T	Drift	Hdg T	Var	Hdg M	GS kt	Dist nm	Time hr/min
Newcastle (55°02'N) (01°41'W)	Carlisle (54°56'N) (02°48'W)	FL60		92	240/25				6W				
Carlisle	Barrow (Walney Island) (54°08'N) (03°16'W)	FL60		91	245/21				6W			Total	

Instructions

1   Time allowed 75 minutes.

2   Fifty multi-choice questions each carrying 2 marks. Marks are not deducted for wrong answers. The pass mark is 70%.

3   Read each question carefully as there is only one answer which is correct.

4   Remember examination technique, you are advised to pass over questions that seem difficult at first sight and return to them when you have answered the others.

1 The major component gasses of the earth's atmosphere are:

A Helium, Nitrogen, Oxygen

B Carbon Dioxide, Hydrogen, Oxygen

C Nitrogen, Water vapour, Oxygen

2 The International Standard Atmosphere is:

A Sea level pressure 1013.2 mb, temperature +15°C, Lapse rate 1.98°C per 1,000', Density 1226 g/m^3

B Sea level pressure 1013.2 mb, temperature 0°C, Lapse rate 1.98°C per 1,000', Density 1226 g/m^3

C Sea level pressure 1013.2 mb, Temperature + 15°C Lapse rate and density do not apply

3 Warm air has the ability to:

A Hold more water vapour than cool air

B Have a higher relative humidity

C Have a lower relative humidity

4 You have calculated the take off distance required based on sea level, ISA conditions. The actual conditions are a pressure altitude of 5,000' and a temperature of +20°C. Which of the following is correct?

A Density is less and take off distance will be reduced

B Density altitude is higher and take off distance will be greater

C Density altitude is lower and take off distance will be greater

5 At the stall, the centre of pressure:

A Moves forward

B Disappears

C Moves aft of the centre of gravity

6 Flaps, in the take-off configuration:

A Increase lift, decrease drag

B Increase lift and drag a little

C Increase lift only

7 At the point of stall, use of ailerons:

A May stall one wing

B Has no effect due to the low airspeed

C Will work as normal

8 Ailerons control the aircraft:

A Around the lateral axis in the longitudinal plane

B Around the longitudinal axis in the lateral plane

C Around the lateral axis in the lateral plane

9 The stalling speed in a steep turn is:

A Decreased

B Increased

C Same as for level flight

10 In a level left hand turn:

A The right hand wing has a higher angle of attack due to its higher speed

B The angle of attack on both wings is the same

C The left hand wing has a higher angle of attack due to it's lower speed

11 Compared to the wings of a jet fighter, the wings of a glider have:

A A low aspect ratio

B A high aspect ratio

C The same aspect ratio

12 If the aircraft is flying "nose heavy":

A The trim wheel must be wound backwards to trim for level flight

B The trailing edge of the trim tab will move down

C The trailing edge of the trim tab will move up

13 "Wash out" on an aeroplane wing is:

A Reduction of angle of incidence towards the tip

B Reduction of angle of incidence towards the fuselage

C Designed to stall the wing tips first to increase stability in the stall

14 The fin on an aeroplane:

A Helps turn the aeroplane

B Balances the weight of the engine

C Assists directional stability

15 Carburettor icing is most likely:

A Temperature 0°C, relative humidity 10%

B Temperature -5°C, relative humidity 30%

C Temperature +12°C, relative humidity 95%

16 The mixture control:

A Must be used above 5,000'

B Should be used in accordance with the manufacturers' instructions

C Can be used at any height

17 To improve take-off performance:

A A fine-pitch propeller is used

B A coarse-pitch propeller is used

C One extra blade is added to the propeller

18 In the carburettor, the throttle directly controls:

A The fuel flow

B The fuel/air flow

C The air flow

19 Whilst checking the magnetos, no decrease in revs is noted:

A This is because of good timing

B The aircraft should not be flown, as the magnetos may be permanently live

C One magneto is not working

20 To be absolutely certain that the magnetos are off:

A The battery master must be off

B It is impossible to be certain they are off, exercise caution at all times

C The keys must be out of the switch

21 Once a circuit breaker has popped:

A 2 minutes must elapse before resetting

B It can be reset immediately

C Do not reset it

22 The primary source of electrical power on a single engined aircraft is:

A The battery

B The generator or alternator

C The magnetos

23 If a fuse blows during flight:

A It should not be replaced until the aircraft has landed

B It should be replaced with one of a higher rating to ensure it will not blow again

C It should be replaced in the air with one of the same rating, but only once

24 If the alternator or generator fails during flight:

A The battery will supply all the electrical loads so the flight can continue

B The master switch should be turned off, and the flight continued

C Electrical loads should be reduced to the bare minimum and a landing made as soon as possible

25 An aircraft has CG limits of 83 - 93 inches aft of the datum. The aircraft is loaded so that the actual CG is 83.5 inches aft of the datum. Compared with a CG position of 92.5 inches aft of the datum the effect on stalling speed and the flare for landing is:

A The stall speed is increased and elevator forces will be light in the flare

B The stall speed is decreased and elevator forces will be light in the flare

C The stall speed is increased and elevator forces will be high in the flare

26 It is important to check that you have gyro suction for the following instruments to operate:

A Altimeter, D.I., Turn and slip

B D.I., Artificial horizon

C Turn and slip, D.I., Artificial horizon

27 The ball in the turn and slip indicator shows the:

A Slip and skid

B Rate of turn

C The aircraft bank angle

28 The following instrument is connected to the pitot pressure source:

A Vertical speed indicator

B Altimeter

C Airspeed indicator

29 The ratio of aerodynamic forces (e.g. total lift) to the aircraft's actual weight is:

A The angle of attack factor

B The load factor

C The krypton factor

30 The directional gyro in a light aircraft:

A Is always aligned to Magnetic North

B Requires re-adjustment by the pilot at regular intervals

C Does not require re-adjustment as it is linked with the compass

31 You wish to operate a UK registered aircraft on MOGAS, where will you find authoritative information concerning such operation:

A In the aircraft's flight manual

B In an AIC

C In a CAA Airworthiness Directive

32 A vacuum pump operates the vacuum driven instruments by:

A Drawing air through the instruments to turn the rotors

B Blowing air through the instruments to turn the rotors

C Sucking against diaphragms in the associated instruments

33 A normal vacuum gauge reading is:

A 3.5 to 4.5 psi

B 4.5 to 5.5 inches of mercury

C 5.5 to 6.5 psi

34 The following instruments are connected to a static pressure source:

A Turn and slip, Artificial horizon, Airspeed indicator

B Altimeter, Vertical speed indicator, Airspeed indicator

C D.I., Vertical speed indicator, Airspeed indicator

35 The shock of heavy taxying loads and landings are primarily absorbed by:

A The main wheel tyres

B The structure of the aircraft

C The landing gear shock absorber

36 Wheel brakes should be tested:

A After starting to taxi

B Just prior to the take-off roll

C Just after landing

37 Oil leakage from an oleo pneumatic shock strut:

A Is not acceptable owing to the limited quantity of oil in the strut

B Is acceptable as this is the means of lubricating the seals

C Is acceptable providing the strut remains at its correct extension

38 On a single engined aircraft, hot air for cabin heating is supplied from:

A The heat exchanger which also supplies heat to the carburettor

B A heat exchanger having exhaust gasses passing the outside of it

C A heat exchanger fitted externally to part of the engine exhaust system and having the exhaust passing through it

39 Cool air ventilators derive their supply of air from:

A Rearwards facing scoops

B Scoops facing into the main airflow

C An air intake under the engine cowling

40 The total weight/moment combination which is within limits in the utility category is:

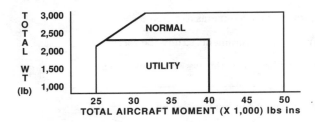

A 2,500 lbs and moment 50,000 lb ins.

B 1,700 lbs and moment 36,000 lb ins.

C 1,500 lbs and moment 42,000 lb ins.

41 If an aircraft is fully loaded with passengers and their baggage:

A The full fuel load may be carried

B The fuel loading is worked out separately

C The fuel load may have to be restricted

42 The ideal fuel/air mixture for efficient aero engine operation is:

A 15 parts air to 15 parts fuel (15:15)

B 15 parts fuel to 1 part air (15:1)

C 1 part fuel to 15 parts air (1:15)

43 After engine starting the oil pressure should register within the green arc within a certain time, or the engine must be shut down immediately. The time allowed is normally:

A 10 seconds

B 30 seconds

C 2 minutes

44 If Carbon Monoxide Gas enters the cabin, it:

A Can be identified by its black colour

B May be identified by its strong smell

C May not be identified because it is colourless and odourless

45 The use of an excessively weak (too lean) mixture at a high power setting can lead to:

A Spark plug fouling (the build up of oil or lead deposits on the spark plugs)

B Detonation (an 'explosive' combustion of the fuel air mixture in the cylinder)

C Carburettor Icing (the formation of ice within the carburettor)

46 Under the Light Aircraft Maintenance Schedule, (LAMS) the Certificate of Airworthiness is valid for:

A 1 year

B 2 years

C 3 years

47 When testing the fuel system for water, using a fuel tester, water may appear as:

A Coloured bubbles in the fuel tester

B Clear bubbles at the top of the fuel sample

C Clear bubbles at the bottom of the fuel sample

48 The person responsible for ensuring that the aircraft is not over-loaded and that the load has been properly secured is the:

A The person loading the aircraft

B The Chief Flying Instructor or his representative

C The commander of the aircraft for the flight

49 When pulling out of a dive, to prevent excessive structural loading on the airframe, the correct action is:

A Gentle back pressure on the control column, together with steady application of engine power as required

B Reduce engine power before gently easing out of the dive

C No action is required as prevention is obtained from the design of the control surfaces

50 Whilst in flight, a drop in RPM occurs, and you suspect carb. ice. However, on applying hot air, the engine initially runs more roughly. You should:

A Return the Carb. heat to cold

B Return the Carb. heat to cold and apply power as the plugs are fouled

C Leave the Carb. heat in hot

1 The Standard Sea Level Pressure is:

A   1031 mb

B   1013.2 mb

C   1003.2 mb

2 The rate of decrease of temperature with height in the ISA is:

A   approx. 2°C per 1,000'

B   approx. 3°C per 1,000'

C   approx. 5°C per 1,000'

3 Temperature and pressure remaining constant, an increase in humidity will cause:

A   A decrease in density

B   An increase in density

C   The density will be unchanged

4 During a pre-flight inspection you notice that a tyre tread has worn to within 4mm of the bottom of the pattern:

A   This is acceptable

B   This is unacceptable, the flight should be cancelled

C   This is acceptable only for operation from a hard runway

5 The lift produced by an aerofoil is due to:

A   An increase in the speed of airflow over the upper surface, resulting in a decrease in pressure, and a decrease in the speed of airflow past the under-surface, resulting in a decrease in pressure.

B   An increase in the speed of airflow over the upper surface, resulting in a decrease in pressure and an increase in the speed of airflow past the under-surface resulting in an increase in pressure.

C   An increase in the speed of airflow over the upper surface, resulting in a decrease in pressure, and a smaller increase in the speed of airflow past the under-surface, resulting in a smaller decrease in pressure.

6 The Centre of Pressure (C of P) is:

A   The point on the aerofoil chord-line through which the resultant of all the aerofoil lifting forces act

B   The point at which the four forces acting on an aircraft are said to act

C   The point at which the entire weight of the aircraft is balanced.

7 In straight and level flight, with the resultant force of the tailplane and elevators acting in an upward direction, the position of the centre of pressure in relation to the centre of gravity must be:

A   In front

B   Behind

C   Located at the same point

8 The lift resulting from the airflow over the top surface of an aerofoil, compared with the lift produced from the airflow past the lower surface is:

A Greater than

B Less than

C Equal to

9 If the angle of attack of an aerofoil is increased slightly, the Centre of Pressure will:

A Move forwards

B Move rearwards

C Remain steady

10 VNE is:

A The maximum indicated airspeed at which manoeuvres may be carried out

B The maximum indicated airspeed at which the aircraft may be flown in any circumstance

C The maximum indicated airspeed at which the aircraft may be flown in level flight, and may be exceeded during certain manoeuvres.

11 Dihedral is:

A The angle between the mainplane and the longitudinal axis

B The angle between the mainplane and the normal axis

C The upward and outward inclination of the mainplane to the horizontal.

12 Split flaps:

A Increase lift and decrease drag during take-off

B Increase drag without increasing lift appreciably when moved from the mid to the fully down position

C Increase lift by increasing the wing area.

13 High Wing Loading will:

A Increase the stalling speed, the landing run, and the landing speed

B Increase the lift, stalling speed and drag

C Decrease the stalling speed, the landing run and landing speed.

14 The Chord line of an aerofoil is :

A A straight line through the Centres of curvature at the leading and trailing edges of the aerofoil section

B A line joining the leading and trailing edges of the aerofoil section, each point of which is equidistant from the upper and lower boundaries of the aerofoil section

C A straight line which touches the curvature of the top surface at the leading and trailing edges tangentially.

15 An aircraft fitted with a variable incidence tailplane and which is flying with a nose up tendency, is corrected by:

A Lowering the leading edge of the tailplane

B Raising the leading edge of the tailplane

C Moving the trim control backwards.

16 Dihedral provides:

A Lateral stability

B Horizontal stability

C Directional stability

17 Induced drag is caused by:

A The difference in pressure between the upper and lower surfaces of an aerofoil

B The twisting motion of the slipstream acting on one side of the fuselage

C The friction between the air and the aircraft surface.

18 If the elevators are moved the aircraft:

A Pitches

B Rolls

C Yaws

19 The aspect ratio of an aerofoil is:

A The ratio of mean camber to span

B The ratio of span to fuselage length

C $\dfrac{\text{Span}}{\text{Mean Chord}}$

20 When airspeed is reduced:

A Parasite and induced drag will reduce

B Parasite drag will increase and induced drag will reduce

C Parasite drag will reduce and induced drag will increase

21 Frise ailerons provide:

A An increase in the yawing moment required for an aircraft to turn due to an increase in the rolling moment

B A reduction in the yawing moment which opposes the tendency of an aircraft to turn

C A reduction in the yawing moment which complements the tendency of an aircraft to turn

22 After engine starting the starter warning light remains lit, this means:

A There is a risk of imminent serious electrical system damage

B The light is faulty and should be reported after the flight

C The starter system is faulty, it should be checked before the next start

23 To prevent flutter the control surfaces are fitted with:

A Inset hinges

B Mass balance

C Spring tabs

24 A control surface fitted with a horn balance is said to be:

A Mass balanced

B Aerodynamically balanced

C Pressure balanced

25 Aerodynamic balancing of control surfaces is necessary to:

A Eliminate control surface flutter

B Assist the pilot to move control surfaces

C Limit the range of movement of control surfaces

26 The range of movement of a control surface is limited by:

A Cables, which must be correctly tensioned

B Control Stops, which are provided in the system

C Control surfaces which are mass balanced

27 If the vent pipe to an aircraft fuel tank became blocked, it would:

A Create a higher pressure on the fuel in the tank, thus disrupting supply to the engine

B Create a lower pressure on the fuel in the tank, thus disrupting supply to the engine

C Make no difference to the fuel supply

28 The oil temperature gauge indicates the temperature of the oil:

A Being delivered to the engine

B In the oil tank

C At the oil cooler

29 In a 60° angle of bank turn an aircraft stalls at 60 knots. In level flight what would you expect the stalling speed to be?

A 60 knots

B 45 knots

C 65 knots

30 Cylinder head temperature can be reduced by:

A Enriching the mixture

B Weakening the mixture

C Decreasing the airspeed

31 Detonation in the engine cylinders can only occur during:

A   The compression stroke

B   The power stroke

C   The induction stroke

32 An aircraft gliding at the recommended best range of glide airspeed, can cover 5 nm from an altitude of 5,000 ft in still air. Its lift/drag ratio is approximately:

A   10:1

B   6:1

C   1:10

33 On a normally aspirated engine fitted with a fixed pitch propeller, carburettor icing is accompanied by:

A   A fall in RPM

B   A rise in RPM

C   A rise in RPM together with a fall in oil temperature

34 If airspeed is reduced, one option to maintain lift is:

A   Increase angle of attack

B   Reduce weight

C   Reduce drag

35 The voltmetre in the cockpit indicates:

A   The voltage in the generator circuit

B   The voltage off load

C   The voltage with the existing load

36 Battery serviceability is tested by:

A   An ammeter

B   A hydrometer

C   An Ohm-meter

37 A circuit breaker that has tripped due to over-load:

A   Can be reset but must not be held in

B   Can be reset and may be held in

C   Cannot be reset

38 At 3,000' an aircraft stalls at 40 knots IAS. At 15,000' the aircraft will stall at:

A   52 knots IAS

B   28 knots IAS

C   40 knots IAS

39 The most reliable instrument indication to determine the direction of a spin is:

A The turn needle / aircraft symbol solely

B The turn needle / aircraft symbol if it agrees with the slip ball

C The heading indicator

40 If in flight you use the rudder solely to turn the aircraft the effect will be:

A Excessive yaw, followed by roll

B Your passenger will begin to look ill!

C Both of the above

41 Water in the pipe work of the pitot/static system:

A Is a problem, as it may freeze and block the system

B Is not a problem, as the system will filter water

C Does not occcur and so is not a problem

42 The high tension voltage of a magneto is produced by:

A Boosting the supply from the generator

B The rapid discharge from an electrical condenser

C Inducing a current between the primary and secondary windings of a coil

43 Compression ratio is:

A The rate at which air ignites in a diesel engine

B The ratio of cylinder volume with the piston at Bottom Dead Centre, to the cylinder volume with the piston at Top Dead Centre

C The ratio of the volume of one cylinder to the volume of all that engine's cylinders

44 An aircraft must be loaded so that the total fuel moment does not exceed 129.6 kg/m. The fuel lever arm is 1.2 m. Assuming a specific gravity of 0.72, how many litres of fuel can be loaded?

A 108 litres

B 150 litres

C 77 litres

45 A right handed propeller is one which:

A Rotates clockwise when viewed from behind the aircraft

B Rotates clockwise when viewed from in front of the aircraft

C Rotates in the same direction as the crankshaft of the engine

46 Running a piston engine at idling RPM for an excessive period can lead to:

A Plug fouling

B Excessive cooling of the cylinders

C The engine burning too much oil

47 A turnbuckle is considered to be safe only when:

A The inspection hole of the cable end fitting is obscured by the tension rod thread

B The inspection hole of the cable end fitting is not obscured by the tension rod thread

C More than three threads of the tension rod threads are visible

48 If the specific gravity of a fuel is 0.72 the weight of 100 imperial gallons of that fuel would be:

A 72 lbs

B 720 lbs

C 7,200 lbs

49 With reference to the weight and balance shown, the combination of weight and total moment with which it would be safe to fly is:

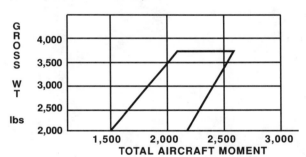

A 3,000 lbs and a moment of 2,500

B 3,500 lbs and a moment of 1,900

C 3,500 lbs and a moment of 2,500

50 Maintenance carried out by a Private Pilot as per the Air Navigation Order (General) regulations for an aircraft with category C of A:

A Must be recorded in the appropriate aircraft log book and signed by the pilot

B Must be recorded in the aircraft log book and certified by a licenced engineer

C Must be recorded on a separate record and produced to the CAA for inspection

1 The force that acts in opposition to thrust is:

A Lift

B Drag

C Weight

2 In level flight the lift force is .... drag force.

A Greater than

B Smaller than

C Equal to

3 An aircraft weighs 2500 lbs and has a wing area of 155ft^2, what is its wing loading?

A 16lbs/ft^2

B 0.062lbs/ft^2

C 32lbs/ft^2

4 The airflow over the top surface of an aerofoil produces:

A A greater proportion of the total lift than the airflow past the lower surface

B An equal proportion of the total to that produced by the airflow past the lower surface

C A smaller proportion of the total lift than the airflow past the lower surface.

5 The induced drag of an aircraft is:

A The drag due to the surface roughness

B The drag due to the frontal area

C The drag due to the lift being produced

6 For an aircraft in level flight, if the wing C of P is AFT of the C G and there is no thrust/drag couple, the tailplane load must be:

A Upward

B Downward

C Zero

7 If the centre of gravity is moved rearward, the longitudinal stability:

A Will be improved

B Will not be affected

C Will be impaired

8 A frise aileron would be used:

A To reduce to yawing moment opposing the turn

B To give an increased rate of roll

C To reduce drag on the inner wing in a turn

9 If a trim tab is operated in flight:

A It will provide aerodynamic forces which will cause the control surface to move

B It will provide aerodynamic force but the control surface will not move

C The tab will only move when the control surface has moved

10 Controls are mass balanced in order to:

A Aerodynamically assist the pilot in moving the controls

B Eliminate control flutter

C Provide equal control forces on all the controls

11 The angle of attack is:

A The angle between the chord and the longitudinal axis

B The angle between the wing and lateral axis

C The angle between the chord and the direction of the relative airflow

12 Washout is:

A An increase of incidence from wing root to tip

B A decrease of chord from wing root to tip

C A decrease of incidence from wing root to tip

13 Longitudinal control is obtained by:

A Ailerons

B Elevators

C Rudder

14 Yawing is a rotation about the:

A Normal axis

B Lateral axis

C Longitudinal axis

15 If the angle of attack is increased, the centre of pressure will:

A Move rearward

B Move forward

C Remain stationary

16 'Lift/Drag' ratio:

A Can be used to describe the aerodynamic efficiency of the wing

B Varies with the angle of attack

C Both of the above

17 Within a four stroke engine, during a complete 'Otto' cycle:

A The inlet valve opens once, the exhaust valve opens twice

B The inlet valve opens once, the exhaust valve opens once

C The inlet valve opens twice, the exhaust valve opens once

18 When power is applied in an aeroplane fitted with a propeller that turns clockwise when viewed from behind, the aeroplane will tend to YAW .... and ROLL...........

A Left, right

B Right, right

C Left, left

19 A fuel load of 270 litres, with a specific gravity of 0.75, gives a total moment of 194.4 kg/m. The lever arm for this load is:

A 0.96

B 1.96

C 9.60

20 The downgoing aileron (ie on the rising wing) moves into an area of .... pressure and will experience .... drag than the other aileron.

A Higher, less

B Higher, more

C Lower, less

21 Adverse aileron yaw is:

A Aileron drag that yaws the nose away from a turn, as the A/C is banked

B Aileron drag that yaws the nose into a turn, as the A/C is banked

C Neither of the above

22 If differential ailerons are used to counteract the effect of adverse aileron yaw, one aileron rises by an amount .... the other aileron is lowered.

A Greater than

B Less than

C The same as

23 Magnetos derive their power from:

A The alternator (unless it fails, in which case the battery)

B The battery (if the alternator is not working)

C The rotation of the engine crankshaft

24 Aerodynamic balances designed to assist a pilot in deflecting a flight control surface may be:

A A trim tab

B A balance tab or some part of the surface placed ahead of the hinge line

C A mass placed foward of the hinge line

25 If the elevator is moved in the pre flight external inspection, then the balance tab should:

A Move in the same direction

B Move in the opposite direction

C Not move

26 When making an over-water flight:

A Life jackets should be worn, inflated

B Life jackets should be worn and inflated once over the sea

C Life jackets should be worn , uninflated

27 With the flaps lowered, the stalling speed will

A Increase

B Decrease

C Increase, but occur at a higher angle of attack

28 Lowering flaps usually produces a pitch change due to:

A Movement of centre of pressure

B Movement of centre of gravity

C Movement of centre of incidence

29 The ammeter indicates:

A The charging rate of the battery

B The load being placed on the alternator

C It varies between aircraft types

30 In a glide, the lift force is:

A Less than the weight

B Greater than the weight

C Equal to the weight

31 In a climb at a steady speed, the thrust is:

A Exactly equal to the drag

B Greater than the drag

C Less than the drag

32 During a turn the lift force is resolved into two forces, these are:

A Centripetal force and a force equal and opposite drag

B Centripetal force and a force equal and opposite weight

C Centripetal force and a force equal and opposite thrust

33 In a co-ordinated, 60 degree angle of bank turn maintaining level flight, what is the approximate increase in stalling airspeed?

A 100 %

B 41%

C 60 %

34 An aircraft is constructed with dihedral to provide:

A Lateral stability about the longitudinal axis

B Longitudinal stability about the lateral axis

C Lateral stability about the normal axis

35 Fuel tanks are vented:

A To allow excess fuel to be vented overboard when filling the tanks

B To allow for expansion of the fuel with change of temperature

C So that as fuel is consumed, the pressure above the fuel will not fall below atmospheric pressure

36 At low temperatures lubricating oil:

A Becomes less viscous

B Becomes more viscous

C Has no change of viscosity

37 Prolonged use of a weak mixture:

A May cause high cylinder head temperatures

B Will increase the fuel consumption

C May cause the engine to run below normal temperature

38 Application of carburettor heat:

A Reduces engine power

B Has no effect on engine power

C Increases engine power because of better volumetric efficiency

39 You have been practising glide approaches to runway 27 when the surface wind was calm. The next day you practice glide approaches to the same runway, the surface wind is 260/18 knots. On the second day you should start the glide approach nearer to the runway and:

A The rate of descent will be greater

B The rate of descent will be less but the approach angle will be steeper

C The rate of descent will be unchanged

40 When entering a spin to the left the down going (left) wing:

A Has a higher angle of attack than the right, but less drag

B Has a higher angle of attack than the right , and more drag

C Has the same angle of attack and drag as the right

41 Disregarding the effects of the wind, the best glide angle will be obtained by gliding at:

A A speed 10% above the stalling speed

B The airspeed which gives the maximum lift/drag ratio

C Gliding at the normal cruising speed

42 The colour of 100LL fuel is:

A Blue

B Clear

C Red

43 In wings-level flight, an aircraft has a stalling speed of 45 knots. To find the expected stalling speed in a 60 degree banked turn maintaining level flight, you should:

A Add 45 knots to 1.41

B Divide 45 knots by 1.41

C Multiply 45 knots by 1.41

44 In a light aircraft, the vacuum pump is most likely to be:

A Electrically driven

B Engine driven

C Hydraulically driven

45 As aircraft weight is increased:

A Take off distance is increased, stall speed is unchanged

B Landing distance is increased, maximum range is unchanged

C Rate of climb is reduced, stall speed is increased

46 You have two batteries, each of 12 volts and 30 ampere-hour capacity. You want to connect these batteries to provide a capacity of 30 ampere hours, the batteries should be connected:

A In series

B In parallel

C In the twilight zone

47 The time remaining to the next major inspection can be determined by:

A The certificate of airworthiness

B The certificate of maintenance review

C The flight manual

48 You are calculating the take-off performance from Le Puy airfield (elevation of 2730 feet), where the air temperature is + 14°C and the QNH is 1013 mb. You already know the calculated take-off performance from Shoreham airfield (elevation 7 feet) in ISA conditions. Which of the following statements is true:

A Density at Le Puy is less than at Shoreham, temperature deviation from ISA is - 1°C, take-off distance will be longer

B Density at Le Puy is the same as at Shoreham, temperature deviation from ISA is 0°C take-off distance will be longer

C Density at Le Puy is less than at Shoreham, temperature deviation from ISA is + 5°C, take-off distance will be longer

49 Take-off distance is measured to:

A The lift off point on the runway

B To 50ft above the runway level

C To 100ft above the runway level

50 An aircraft is fitted with a 'centre-zero' reading ammeter (illustrated). The ammeter is presently indicating:

A A discharge, the battery is supplying all electrical power

B A discharge, the alternator is supplying all electrical power

C A positive charge, the battery is being charged by the alternator at about 5 ampere/hours

1 The International Standard Atmosphere at mean sea level is defined as:

A 1013 mb, +15°C

B 1225 mb, +15°C

C 1013 mb, +25°C

2 The amount of water vapour in the air compared to the maximum that the air could absorb at that temperature is the:

A Water vapour ratio, which is 100% when the air is saturated

B Relative humidity, increased relative humidity reduces density

C Water vapour ratio, which is 1:1 when the air is saturated

3 Usually a aircraft tyre has a painted mark which should align with a similar mark on the wheel centre. This mark is:

A Called the creep mark and measures tyre creep

B Called the pressure mark and helps the pilot to gauge tyre pressure

C Called the tyre mark and helps to measure tyre wear

4 Does the fin give stability:

A Laterally

B Longitudinally

C Directionally

5 An aircraft's nose has a tendency to pitch up. To correct this, should the:

A Elevator be moved down and the trim tab moved down

B Elevator be moved down and the trim tab moved up

C Elevator be moved up and the trim tab moved down

6 In a UK registered light aircraft (less than 2730 KG maximum total authorised weight) a safety belt with a diagonal shoulder strap for the front seat(s) is generally:

A Mandatory if the aircraft has full aerobatic capability

B Advisory, fitted at the pilot's discretion

C Mandatory

7 In relation to stalling angle of attack:

A Use of flaps increases the stalling angle of attack

B Use of slots and slats increases the stalling angle of attack

C Use of flaps or slots and slats does not alter stalling angle of attack

8 About which axis does an aircraft yaw?

A Normal

B Longitudinal

C Lateral

9 What is the purpose of wing 'slats'?

A   To slow the aircraft down

B   To increase the take off speed

C   To delay the stall

10 In what temperature range is carburettor ice most likely to form?

A   +5°C to -25°C

B   -5°C to +25°C

C   -5°C to -25°C

11 What is the cycle of a 4-stroke engine?

A   Induction, compression, ignition, exhaust

B   Compression, induction, ignition, exhaust

C   Induction, ignition, compression, exhaust

12 An aircraft is fitted with a fixed pitch propeller. If the aircraft accelerates in a dive, with a constant throttle setting, will the engine R.P.M.:

A   Increase

B   Decrease

C   Remain the same

13 Why is a propeller blade twisted along its length?

A   To reduce centrifugal stress

B   To reduce propellor torque

C   To maintain a constant angle of attack along the blade.

14 What toxic gas is produced by an aircraft engine?

A   Carbon dioxide

B   Carbon monoxide

C   Nitrogen

15 When should a propellor be treated as 'live' ?

A   When the key is in the ignition.

B   Always.

C   When the master switch is 'on'.

16 If you notice fluid leaking from a nosewheel oleo, should you:

A   Report it, but continue with the planned flight

B   Continue with your planned flight and report the leak afterwards

C   Report the leak immediately and postpone the flight until it is rectified

17 Best lift/drag ratio occurs:

A Just below stalling angle of attack

B Just below 0° angle of attack

C Neither of the above

18 What gas is the main constituent of the earth's atmosphere?

A Nitrogen

B Oxygen

C Carbon dioxide

19 If the primer is left unlocked, what may happen to a running aircraft engine?

A A rich cut

B A weak cut

C Neither of the above

20 What type of fuel is used in a piston engine aircraft?

A Avtur

B Avtag

C Avgas

21 What colour indicates an AVTUR installation?

A Red

B Black

C Yellow

22 Why should the fuel tanks be filled up before parking an aircraft overnight?

A To prevent time being wasted on refuelling in the morning

B To prevent condensation forming in the fuel tanks

C To reduce the risk of a vapour explosion in the fuel tanks

23 Detonation in a piston engine can be caused by:

A An over-lean mixture

B An over-rich mixture

C A cold engine

24 The altimeter is fed by:

A Static pressure

B Pitot pressure

C Dynamic pressure

25 During a descent, the pitot tube becomes blocked, the ASI will subsequently:

A Over - read

B Under - read

C Read correctly

26 During a descent, the static vent becomes blocked, the VSI will indicate:

A A descent

B Zero

C A climb

27 A distribution point for electrical power to various services is known as:

A A bus bar

B A circuit breaker

C A distributor

28 A flight manual includes a CAA supplement. The manual details one method of spin recovery, the supplement another. Do you:

A Abide by the manual

B Abide by the CAA supplement

C Compromise between the two

29 Which of the following are all pressure - fed instruments?

A ASI, VSI, Altimeter

B ASI, Altimeter, DI

C ASI, AI, VSI

30 Towards the end of a landing run (in an aircraft that has mechanical nose-wheel steering), you notice a distinct vibration, felt through the rudder pedals. This vibration is most likely to be:

A Nose wheel shimmy caused by an excessively worn tyre

B Nose wheel shimmy caused by a faulty shimmy damper or torque link

C Nose wheel shimmy caused by excessive differential braking

31 With reference to the balance indicator, an aircraft is turning to the left and the ball is out to the right:

A The aircraft is skidding and too much left rudder has been applied

B The aircraft is skidding and too much right rudder has been applied

C The aircraft is slipping and too much left rudder has been applied

32 A control lock is used:

A To lock the trimmers in a fixed position

B To lock the controls in steady straight and level flight

C To lock the controls when the aircraft is parked

33 Compressing a gas causes its temperature to:

A Increase

B Decrease

C Remain the same

34 The best airspeed to use for obstacle clearance after take off is:

A The best angle of climb airspeed

B The best rate of climb airspeed

C The VFE airspeed

35 Increasing the load carried by an aircraft:

A Increases the angle of attack at which the stall occurs

B Decreases the angle of attack at which the stall occurs

C Does not affect the angle of attack at which the stall occurs

36 Increasing the load carried by an aircraft:

A Increases stall speed

B Decreases stall speed

C Does not affect stall speed

37 The pitot tube senses:

A Static pressure

B Dynamic pressure

C Static and Dynamic pressure

38 An aircraft must always be loaded to remain within the specified centre of gravity limits. If flight is attempted with a C of G that exceeds the aft limit:

A Stall speed is increased and the aircraft will feel tail heavy

B The aircraft is designed not to get airborne

C Control difficulties and possible loss of control of the aircraft may occur

39 An aircraft has a right - hand propeller. Will propeller torque:

A Roll the aircraft to the left

B Roll the aircraft to the right

C Neither of the above are true

40 Which type of fire extinguisher must <u>NOT</u> be used on a petrol or electrical fire?

A Gas

B Dry powder

C Water

41 In a steady climb:

A Thrust = Lift

B Weight = Drag

C Lift is greater than Thrust

42 How many ignition systems does a light aircraft engine normally have?

A 1

B 2

C 3

43 Which of these instruments does the vacuum pump not drive?

A AI

B VSI

C HI

44 Within a typical aircraft float-type carburettor, the main jet (A), and the idling jet (B) perform the following functions:

A (A) Supplies fuel directly into the cylinder (B) Takes over if the main jet becomes blocked

B (A) Supplies fuel into the venturi (B) Controls the supply of fuel to the engine when the throttle valve is almost closed

C (A) Supplies air into the venturi (B) Supplies force-fed air to the venturi when the engine is operating at less than 1000 RPM

45 A pilot has calculated take off and landing performance based on a dry tarmac runway. It transpires that the runway is grass and wet, how will performance be effected?

A Take off and landing distances will be longer

B Take off distance will be longer, landing distance will be shorter

C Take off distance will be longer, landing distance will be the same

46 A duplicate inspection must be carried out by:

A The aircraft's owner and another PPL holder

B The aircraft's owner and a licenced engineer

C Two licenced engineers

47 If you take off from a concrete runway as opposed to your normal grass runway, your take off distance will have:

A Increased

B Decreased

C Remained the same

48 An aircraft is fitted with a 'left-zero' reading ammeter (illustrated). The ammeter is currently indicating:

A The ammeter is supplying zero output

B The battery is fully charged

C The battery is below normal operating temperature

49 For the same airspeed, the angle of attack in a turn:

A Is greater than in straight and level flight

B Is less than in straight and level flight

C Is the same as in straight and level flight

50 A 'stabilator' is:

A A fixed tailplane and movable elevator

B A movable horizontal stabiliser

C A balancing weight on the elevator

Instructions

1   Time allowed 30 minutes.

2   Twenty multi-choice questions each carrying 5 marks. Marks are not deducted for wrong answers. The pass mark is 70%.

3   Read each question carefully as there is only one answer which is correct.

4   Remember examination technique, you are advised to pass over questions that seem difficult at first sight and return to them when you have answered the others.

1 The body maintains a greater store of which of the following gases?

A Oxygen

B Carbon Dioxide

C Carbon Monoxide

2 At altitudes above 10,000' aircrew require additional oxygen. This is due to the fall in?

A Proportion of oxygen

B Temperature of oxygen

C Pressure of oxygen

3 If a crewmember has blue tinged lips and fingers and appears to be breathing rapidly, he is most likely to be suffering from?

A Hyperventilation.

B Hypoxia

C Hypothermia

4 The mechanism that allows the middle ear to match the ambient pressure is:

A The sinuses

B The vestibular apparatus

C The Eustachian tubes

5 The time of useful consciousness at 30,000' is?

A 2-3 minutes

B 45-75 seconds

C 20-30 seconds

6 After swimming with scuba equipment if a depth of 30' has not been exceeded, the recommended time interval before flying is:

A 12 hrs.

B 24 hrs.

C 48 hrs.

7 The parts of the eye that respond best to low light situations are?

A Fovea

B Cones

C Rods

8 Smoking .... the risk of onset of hypoxia in a crew member at altitude.

A Has no effect on

B Reduces

C Increases

9 When carbon monoxide enters the cabin, it can be detected by?

A Its taste

B Its odour

C A carbon monoxide detector

10 Are you fit to fly when suffering from a cold?

A No

B Yes

C Yes, if you have taken non-prescription medicine

11 A seat position lower than the Design Eye Position will?

A Reduce forward visibility on the approach

B Improve forward visibility on the approach

C Have no effect on the visual approach

12 An aircraft on a collision course with yours is most likely to:

A Remain stationary on your aircraft's windscreen

B Move across your aircraft's windscreen

C Not appear on your aircraft's windscreen

13 During a flight in a helicopter in bright overhead sunlight, a passenger complains of a feeling of metal unease and discomfort;

A The passenger may be effected by 'flicker effect', advise him/her to wear sunglasses or to close and cover his/her eyes

B The passenger may be effected by 'flicker effect', advise him/her to cover the adjacent window

C Both A and B can be correct

14 Information in working memory, if not remembered, will be lost in?

A 10 - 20 seconds

B 10 - 20 minutes

C 5 - 10 minutes

15 The most effective lookout technique is to:

A Stare straight ahead

B Move the head from side to side

C Use a regular, practiced, scanning pattern

16 A high level of arousal?

A Improves performance

B Reduces performance

C Has no effect on performance

17 While carrying out duties in the early hours of the morning, a pilot can expect his or her performance?

A To be unaffected

B To improve as the body is more relaxed

C To deteriorate as the body temperature is lowest

18 Narcolepsy is a condition in which a person?

A Is dependent on drugs

B Can be treated with drugs

C Is unable to prevent themselves from falling asleep

19 If a pilot is suffering from gastroenteritis?

A It can be treated and they may fly as normal

B They should not fly

C They can fly providing they do not inform their doctor

20 The body can withstand G-forces of?

A 25 G vertically and 45 G fore and aft

B 6 G vertically and 12 G fore and aft

C 30 G vertically and 10 G fore and aft

1 The body is normally saturated with what gas?

A O_2

B CO_2

C N

2 When a person is deprived of the oxygen they need, they are suffering from:

A Hyperventilation

B Hypoxia

C Hysteresis

3 Suseptability to hypoxia is increased by:

A Cold.

B Heat.

C Inactivity.

4 Prolonged exposure to U.V. light usually damages the:

A Cornea.

B Lens.

C Iris.

5 What is the time of useful conciousness at 18,000ft?

A 2-3 minutes

B 45-75 seconds

C 30 minutes

6 What is the maximum tolerance of negative "G" for the human body?

A -5g

B -3g

C -2g

7 When flying at altitude, you are .... susceptible to CO poisoning.

A More

B Less

C Just as

8 An aircraft on a collision course with yours can be difficult to spot because:

A It is most likely to remain stationary on the windscreen

B It moves quickly across the windscreen

C It may appear at different places on the windscreen

9 How is oxygen transported around the body?

A By white blood cells.

B By carbon dioxide molecules (carbolic acid).

C By Haemoglobin.

10 If 30ft is exceeded when diving using compressed air, you must not fly for:

A 12 hours

B 24 hours

C 48 hours

11 A light aircraft flying at 90 knots is conflicting head on with a military jet flying at 420 knots. approximately how quickly are they closing in terms of seconds per mile?

A 7 seconds per mile

B 10 seconds per mile

C 20 seconds per mile

12 In the example above, if the pilots sight each other at a range of 2 miles, how much time is available to take avoiding action?

A 40 seconds

B 20 seconds

C 14 seconds

13 In relation to a practised lookout scan:

A It will be necessary to adjust the scan to compensate for 'blind spots' caused by the aircraft design and structure

B The aircraft will be designed not to have any 'blind spots'

C An aircraft hidden in a 'blind spot' cannot be on a collision course with you

14 As workload is increased, pilot performance levels:

A Continuously increase.

B Continuously decrease.

C Gradually increase then decrease.

15 Gastroenteritis is most usually caused by:

A Food poisoning

B The common cold

C Hypoxia

16 It is easier to equalise pressure in the middle ear:

A In the climb

B In the descent

C When flying at a faster speed

17 A non-smoker will normally have a carbon monoxide saturation of about 3 %. A smoker may have a carbon monoxide saturation of ...(a)... and so is ...(b)... susceptible to carbon monoxide poisoning.

A (a) 10%   (b) more

B (a) 1 %   (b) less

C (a) 10%   (b) less

18 In order to come to a group decision, a group leader should, preferably:

A Give a clear indication of his/her preferred solution before soliciting the views of other group members.

B Consult other group members before giving his/her own view.

C Identify the best solution him/herself and give clear instructions on carrying out his/her wishes without consulting other group members.

19 When approaching an UPSLOPING runway, pilots may believe they are:

A Too high

B Too low

C Too fast

20 If you receive a local anaesthetic during dental treatment, you are advised not to fly for at least the following:

A 24 hours

B 2 hours

C 12 hours

1 The troposphere is the:

A Inner layer of the atmosphere.

B Middle layer of the atmosphere.

C Outer layer of the atmosphere.

2 The atmosphere contains:

A About 78% oxygen.

B About 21% oxygen.

C About 78% CO

3 Alveoli are:

A Small air sacs in the lungs.

B Small air sacs in the liver.

C Small blood vessels in the lungs.

4 The main function of haemoglobin is to:

A To transport carbon dioxide around the body.

B To expell unwanted carbolic acid.

C To transport oxygen around the body.

5 A rise in carbon dioxide in the blood causes:

A A reduction in the respiration rate.

B An increase in the respiration rate.

C No change in the respiration rate.

6 The altitude at which 100% oxygen has the same partial pressure as the partial pressure of oxygen at ground level is:

A 40,000ft

B 34,000ft

C 22,000ft

7 Exercise:

A Increases oxygen demand and increases the degree of hypoxia.

B Increases blood flow and protects against hypoxia.

C Does not effect the susceptability to hypoxia.

8 What is hypoxia?

A Excess of CO_2

B Excess of nitrogen

C Lack of oxygen

9 As a general rule, flaps should not be raised during the landing because:

A Such action might distract the pilot from the primary task of handling the aircraft

B In a retractable undercarriage aircraft, it is possible to raise the undercarriage by mistake

C Both of the above

10 The eye adapts to differing light levels by:

A Chemical changes in the retina.

B Chemical changes in the pupil.

C The lens becomes progressively opaque.

11 Disease wise, the World's biggest killer is:

A Typhoid

B Hepatitis

C Malaria

12 Body Mass Index (BMI) is calculated by the formulae:

A Weight in Kg divided by height in metres squared.

B Height in metres divided by weight in Kg.

C Weight in Kg divided by height in feet.

13 The BMI figure over which a man can be considered to be overweight is:

A 20

B 25

C 15

14 Approximately how many units of alcohol should be eliminated from the blood in three hours?

A 3 units

B 6 units

C 4 units

15 You receive a general anaesthetic for a minor cosmetic operation. You are advised not to fly for at least the following:

A 24 hours

B 48 hours

C 72 hours

16 Information in long term memory:

A Has an average life of about 1 year.

B Cannot be demonstrated ever to be lost.

C Has an average life of 5 years.

17 The hazardous attitude "macho" can best be characterised by:

A "It won't happen to me"

B "I can do it"

C "Don't tell me"

18 The effect of alcohol

A Increases with increasing altitude.

B Decreases with increasing altitude.

C Is unaffected by decreasing altitude.

19 An approaching aircraft that is on a constant bearing represents:

A Absolutely no risk of collision.

B The least risk of collision.

C The greatest risk of collision.

20 The most important consideration in display layout is:

A Layout

B Colour

C Standardisation

1 Hyperventilation means breathing:

A More deeply and frequently than is necessary.

B Less deeply and frequently than is necessary.

C More deeply but less frequently than necessary.

2 Breathing too rapidly, apprehension or motion sickness could cause:

A Hyperventilation

B Hypoxia

C Hydroxia

3 Long sight not caused by age is called:

A Myopia

B Presbyopia

C Hypermetropia

4 The vision requirement for pilots requires the ability to read a car number plate at about:

A 20 metres

B 30 metres

C 40 metres

5 The concentration of oxygen in the atmosphere:

A Is 78% of the total of all gases present.

B Is highest at ground level.

C Is constant at all altitudes.

6 Donating blood:

A Is permitted subject to at least 24 hours elapsing prior to next flight.

B Is not recommended for aircrew who are actively flying.

C Imposes no restrictions on subsequent flying.

7 Which particular item of pilot equipment is believed to significantly increase accident survivability in the case of flight in aerobatic/open cockpit aircraft:

A A protective helmet

B A flying suit

C A silk scarf

8 Exposure to noise energy for prolonged periods will lead to Noise Induced Hearing Loss (NIHL), specifically amounts in excess of:

A 90 db

B 100 - 120 db

C 70 db

9 With regard to the circadian rhythm of body temperature, at what time is the body temperature at its lowest:

A 06:00

B 03:00

C 05:00

10 'Situational awareness' - the accurate perception of conditions effecting you and your aircraft - is:

A Undesirable, as it 'over-loads' the pilot

B Desirable in a pilot, it means knowing what is happening around you

C Best achieved by concentrating on one aspect to exclusion of all others.

11 Performance on mental arithmetic tasks and verbal reasoning peak around:

A 09:00

B 12:00

C 11:00

12 The greatest number of aviation accidents occur:

A During take off and landing.

B During the cruising phase of flight.

C Whilst flying over mountainous terrain.

13 Which of the following graphs best represent the "Arousal/Performance" graph?

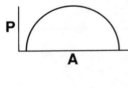 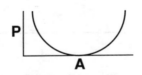 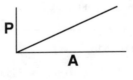

A   B   C

14 Performance is adversely affected by:

A High arousal

B High and low arousal

C Medium arousal

15 If a pilot's seat is too low on the approach, the effect would be to:

A Obscure the whole runway.

B Obscure the overshoot.

C Obscure the undershoot.

16 Referring to the Body Mass Index a 13 stone, 5'8" 35 year old male is regarded as:

A Overweight

B Underweight

C Normal

17 What is the most serious cause of coronary heart disease?

A Smoking

B Family history

C Obesity

18 Generally, a unit of alcohol is taken as being equivalent to:

A 1/2 pint of beer OR a glass of wine OR a single measure of spirit.

B 1 pint of beer OR 2 glasses of wine OR a double measure of spirit.

C 2 pints of beer OR 4 glasses of wine OR a treble measure of spirit.

19 Stress management is:

A The effect, upon a person in a managerial, or other responsible position, of the pressures of the job.

B The process whereby individuals adopt systems to assist in coping with stress.

C The use of some process such as an exercise programme to remove the stress.

20 Which of the following Altimeter dials is the least ambiguous?

  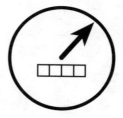

A **B** **C**

1 The time of useful consiousness at 25,000ft is:

A 12 seconds

B 2-3 minutes

C 11 minutes

2 What time, approximately, is required to eliminate two units of alcohol from the blood?

A 1/2 hour

B 1 hour

C 2 hours

3 Does cold increase susceptibility to Hypoxia?

A Yes, because it is necessary to generate more energy which increases the demand for oxygen.

B No. because the body's metabolism slows, reducing the need for oxygen consumption.

C Yes, because the body's metabolism increases.

4 In terms of pilot experience, the accident risk is greatest:

A Between 1000 - 2000 hours

B In the first 100 hours

C Between 200 -500 hours

5 What % of Nitrogen is contained in the atmosphere?

A 70%

B 68%

C 78%

6 Full dark adaptation of cones takes approximately?

A 6 minutes

B 10 minutes

C 7 minutes

7 'Flicker effect', which can cause an epileptic-type fit in a susceptible person, can be caused by:

A Flashing navigation lights

B Helicopter rotor blades, or a windmilling propeller

C A red rotating beacon

8 In an impact, the body can tolerate in the fore and aft axis:

A 45 G

B 25 G

C 60 G

9 The best form of harness is the _____ point system.
(fill in the missing figure)

A 3

B 5

C 4

10 One possible therapy for a passenger suffering from motion sickness is to:

A Close his/her eyes

B Avoid moving his/her head

C Both of the above

11 Which of the following statements concerning 'flicker effect', which can cause an epileptic-type fit in a susceptible person, is the most accurate:

A It can occur in a helicopter or fixed-wing aircraft

B It can only occur in a helicopter

C It cannot occur in an aviation environment

12 A pilot may experience the illusory perception of pitching up when in fact in level flight, when the aircraft is:

A Decelerating

B Accelerating

C Rolling

13 The eye datum of Design eye position is established:

A To enable the pilot to see all his flight instruments with minimum scan movement of the head.

B To determine the eventual size of the Flight deck and where window frames will be positioned so as not to interfere with the pilots field of view.

C So that the pilot can maintain an adequate view of all the important displays inside and of the world outside with minimal head movement.

14 A typical time interval between seeing an aircraft on a collision course and taking avoiding action is:

A 5 seconds

B 2 seconds

C 10 seconds

15 If a stimulus is expected and the response prepared, when an unexpected stimulus is received:

A The mind will freeze and will require the reminder from its data store before actioning the new demand. The prepared response will be transferred to the long-term memory store.

B The prepared response will be transferred to the long term memory store.

C The prepared response is likely to be carried out.

16 A person is considered obese when the Body Mass Index (BMI) is over?

A 30

B 22

C 25

17 A more experienced pilot-in-command should encourage a less experienced co-pilot to:

A Keep quiet, do as told and learn something.

B Discuss any problems after the flight is over.

C Always express any doubts or queries.

18 In Aviation 'Atmospheric Perspective' means:

A A change in the altitude of the aircraft will lead to a possible lengthening or shortening of a runway's apparent length.

B The tendency for objects to become indistinct with distance.

C The presence of a sloping cloud bank may be mistaken for a horizon, causing the pilot who is flying without reference to instruments to bank the aircraft to align it with the cloud bank.

19 The 'Fight or Flight' response occurs:

A When the sympathetic Nervous System provides the person with the resources to cope with a new and sudden source of stress.

B When a normal non-aggressive person suffers as a result of shock, turns and chooses Flight rather than Fight

C When the Parasympathetic Nervous system provides extra resourses to the individual to cope with a sudden new source of stress.

20 The capacity of the working memory may be expanded by:

A Chunking the data.

B Constant repetition of material

C Immediate transfer of the material to the Long-Term memory.

1 The composition of the atmosphere from sea level to about 60,000ft retains proportions of:

A 50% Nitrogen, 40% Oxygen, 10% other gases

B 78% Oxygen, 21% Nitrogen, 1% other gases

C 78% Nitrogen, 21% Oxygen, 1% other gases

2 Oxygen is required by the Human body to:

A Clear the blood of impurities produced by the body

B Derive energy from food by chemical oxidation

C To ensure the conversion of fats and proteins to carbohydrates required for tissue regeneration

3 Taking 1 unit of alcohol to equal 1/2 pint of beer, a man would reach the approximate "damage threshold" at:

A 5 pints per day/20 pints per week

B 6 pints per day/25 pints per week

C 3 pints per day/15 pints per week

4 Whilst re-fuelling an aircraft you spill a significant quantity of aviation fuel onto your skin and adjacent clothing. What should you do?

A Immediately discard the effected clothing and wash the effected skin with cold water

B Nothing, unless you are a smoker

C Nothing, aviation fuel has no known adverse effects in these circumstances

5 The effect of smoking 20 cigarettes a day is to increase the apparent ambient pressure by:

A 5 to 6 thousand feet

B 2 to 3 thousand feet

C 1 to 3 thousand feet

6 The effect of altitude on the gastro-intestinal tract may cause stretching of the small bowel, if gas is present in this part of the system. This possibility may be minimised by:

A Taking mild antacid tablets when the problem first becomes apparent

B Avoiding the foodstuffs which cause the production of intestinal gases

C Ensuring a lifestyle which leads to regular bowel movements

7 A pilot suffering from decompression sickness should:

A Land as soon as possible and seek medical assistance.

B Decrease the cabin pressure to relieve the symptoms.

C Continue the flight at a lower altitude and carry out exercises to relieve any pains in the affected area.

8 At night you are making a visual approach to an isolated airfield, where the runway is well lit but there are few other lights visible:

A There is no danger of optical illusion if you concentrate solely on the runway

B There is an optical illusion that may cause you to approach too fast

C There is an optical illusion that may cause you to approach too low

9 The time of useful conciousness at an altitude of 45,000 ft is:

A 1 minute

B 30 seconds

C 12 seconds

10 The greatest source of incapacipation in flight is:

A Heart attacks

B Severe disorientation

C Acute gastroenteritis

11 A man is considered to be overweight if his body mass index is over:

A 30

B 25

C 20

12 The greatest percentage of aviation accidents can be attributed to:

A Pilot error

B Mechanical failure

C Factors outside the control of the pilot

13 A light twin with an airspeed of 160 knots is conflicting head on with a military jet whose airspeed is 450 knots. If the pilots see each other at a range of 2 nm, how much time is available to react?

A 12 seconds

B 20 seconds

C 30 seconds

14 Side-by-side seating promotes:

A Confrontation

B Co-operation

C Hostility

15 If leading a group, you should whenever possible:

A Show independence and competence by solving problems without consulting other group members

B Argue strongly for your own point of view in order to maintain authority, even if you are not sure that you are right

C Seek the views of other group members before making a decision

16 The approximate threshold for alcohol intake above which physical damage may be sustained is:

A The same for men and women

B Higher for women than for men

C Higher for men than women

17 During a night flight, you are advised of conflicting traffic in your 12 o'clock. For the best chance of spotting the traffic you should look:

A About 10 degrees either side of dead-ahead

B Dead-ahead

C It depends on the aircraft's heading

18 To increase the value of a displayed variable, an associated knob should turn:

A Anticlockwise

B In either direction

C Clockwise

19 When the eyes are at rest, they tend to focus:

A At infinity

B At 2-3 metres ahead

C It depends on age

20 In the late stages of an approach, how is the ground proximity judged?

A Texture and relative speed of ground features

B Colour and contrast of ground features

C Position of aircraft nose, relative to the horizon

1 The approximate period of useful consciousness at 30,000ft is:

A   15 seconds

B   1 minute

C   2-3 minutes

2 If disorientated the pilot should believe:

A   Vision and inner ear

B   Cochlea

C   Instruments

3 Required oxygen can be provided at 37,000ft by breathing:

A   100% oxygen under pressure

B   100% oxygen

C   An oxygen/air mixture

4 The Sinuses can vent gas more easily:

A   On ascent

B   On descent

C   With a cold

5 In short duration acceleration/deceleration the body can tolerate up to .... G in the fore/aft axis:

A   25

B   15

C   45

6 The capacity of the eye to resolve details is termed:

A   Acuity

B   Accommodation

C   Retinal focusing

7 For men damaging levels of alcohol occur when more than a specified intake is exceeded. The limit is:

A   6 units daily

B   40 units weekly

C   4 units daily

8 A pilot who is 35 years old has a weight of 80kg and is 165cm. His Body Mass Index is:

A   23 about right

B   29 overweight

C   36 obese

9 Smoking, or alcohol in the blood

A Has no effect on night vision

B Decreases night vision

C Increases night vision

10 If a pilot is seated below the design eye point (DEP) during an approach, at about 200ft he/she will:

A Lose sight of a portion of the overshoot

B See more than if seated at the DEP

C Lose sight of a portion of the undershoot

11 During flight you have been trained to consider all input, to constantly up-date your situation and to plan ahead. This desirable action is known as:

A Situational awareness

B Conformality

C Convergence

12 Accidents caused by colliding with high ground, or losing control, in cloud/poor weather:

A Account for a large percentage of accident statistics

B Are usually completely avoidable

C Both of the above

13 Time of useful consciousness at altitude is:

A Increased by sitting quietly

B Increased by moderate activity

C Not effected by activity

14 Confirmation bias:

A Makes the pilot look for the most obvious solution to a problem to avoid using the full checklist

B Is the re-inforcement of any idea by any past experience of a similar problem

C Tends to make the pilot accept information that confirms his/her diagnosis of a problem and reject information that does not fit into his/her theory

15 Referring to the diagram below, where does optimal arousal occur:

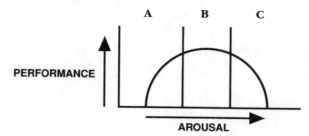

16 Particularly to an inexperienced passenger, a difference between the messages the brain receives from the eyes and from the ears can lead to:

A Motion sickness

B Altitude sickness

C Anoxia

17 Hyperventilation is:

A The number one cause of in-flight incapacitation

B A condition brought on by lack of oxygen

C A condition brought on by having too little carbon dioxide in the lungs

18 If a pilot experiences "spatial disorienation" whilst flying on instruments, the best solution is to:

A Trust the senses

B Request ATC assistance

C Refer to, and believe in, the flight instruments

19 In the cockpit of a 'complex' single engine aircraft:

A The undercarriage and flap controls should look and feel the same

B The undercarriage and flap controls should look and feel different

C The undercarriage and flap controls should be next to each other

20 A circular instrument with fixed scale and moving pointer is:

A An analogue display instrument

B Poor for displaying bearing information

C Ideal for displaying range information

1 A pilot showing symptoms of dizziness, tingling at the fingertips and blurred vision may be suffering from:

A Hypoxia

B Anoxia

C Hyperventilation

2 When approaching a runway wider than the pilot is used to, the aircraft will appear to be:

A At too slow an airspeed

B Low on the approach

C On the correct approach slope

3 For effective lookout scanning it is necessary to:

A Focus at a nearby object

B Focus on a distant object

C Allow the eyes to rest

4 The CAA recommend that breathing apparatus is used when operating above:

A above 5000 feet

B above 8000 feet

C above 10000 feet

5 Long duration acceleration causes 'greying out' of vision and ultimately unconsciousness in the relaxed subject, at approximately:

A 4.5G

B 3.5G

C 5.0G

6 Hyperventilation is best overcome by:

A Increasing stress levels, and moderate activity.

B Stopping the use of supplemental oxygen.

C Breathing normally.

7 The number one cause of serious accidents to light aircraft is:

A Loss of control/stall-spin

B Mid-air collisions

C Pilot incapacitation or physical unfitness for flight

8 The symptoms of headaches, breathlessness, impaired judgement and eventual loss of consciousness pertain to which gas?

A O_2

B CO_2

C CO

9 Full dark adaptation of the cones takes approximately:

A 30 minutes

B 7 minutes

C 5 minutes

10 If an emergency occurs in flight, the best course of action is to:

A Request ATC assistance.

B Act immediately, using the emergency checklist.

C Assess the situation, consider the options and then choose the appropiate course of action.

11 Flying with a "hangover", but more than 12 hours after last drinking alcohol:

A Is considered safe at low altitudes.

B Is permitted for 2 crew operations.

C Increases the chance of committing errors.

12 One of the classes of stress is cognitive stress, cognitive effects can be identified as:

A Sleep disorders, increased heart rate and dry mouth

B Fatigue, Apathy, Anxiety

C Forgetfulness, lack of concentration, difficulty in switching off

13 Drinking excessive amounts of tea and coffee before, or during, flight can lead to:

A Distracting desire to empty bladder, with consequent loss of concentration.

B Tiredness, muscle tremors and stomach irritation.

C Both of the above.

14 The main personality problem in single pilot operations is:

A Failures of perception

B Errors of skill

C Risk taking

15 The hazardous attitude that is best summed up in the phrase "it won't happen to me" is:

A Anti- authority

B Resignation

C Invulnerability

16 Whilst turning, a high wing aircraft,

A Has better visibility 'into' the turn.

B Has better visibility behind.

C Has better visibility 'out of' the turn.

17 Approximately how many units of alcohol should be eliminated from the blood in 1 hour?

A 2 units

B 1 unit

C 4 units

18 When using supplemental oxygen in-flight:

A Smoking is permitted

B Smoking is not permitted

C Smoking by passengers only is permitted

19 A pilot is most likely to experience the illusory perception of "pitching up" during

A The landing roll

B The beginning of descent from cruise

C A go-around

20 Yellow used in a display signifies:

A Advisory information

B An alert

C Non- critical functions

1 At 30,000ft the percentage of oxygen present in the atmosphere is:

A 78%

B Dependent on ambient pressure

C 21%

2 Light levels at high altitude are dangerous because they:

A Contain more of the damaging blue and UV light

B Cause the iris to close, blinding the pilot

C They are not dangerous

3 When on collision course with another aircraft, that aircraft will appear to:

A Grow bigger at a constant rate

B Grow bigger slowly, and then grow bigger rapidly at close range

C Remain at a constant image size

4 When a pilot is being subjected to prolonged positive "G" loading, above 3-4 G, an early symptom of impending unconsciouness is:

A Red-out

B Greying out - partial loss of vision

C Loss of hearing

5 A major function of the inner ear is:

A To detect angular and linear accelerations of the head

B To prevent direct sound damaging the otoliths

C To connect the ear to the nasal passage

6 The most obvious symptom of a person suffering from carbon monoxide poisoning is:

B The will have blue lips and finger tips

B Muscular impairment

C They will have cherry red lips and flushed cheeks

7 Yellow fever vaccine is effective for at least:

A 6 months

B 10 years

C 2 years

8 For a healthy individual, hypoglycaemia can best be avoided by:

A Eating regularly, and supplementing with glucose containing sweets or sweet drinks.

B Reducing alcohol intake

C Maintaining a comfortable cabin temperature

9 Decompression sickness (DCS) is caused by:

A Nitrogen coming out of solution in the blood to form bubbles in body tissues:

B A rapid loss of pressurisation in the cabin

C Pains in the shoulder and elbow

10 When a collision course with an aircraft on a reciprocal track, the size of the approaching aircraft:

A Increases gradually and is therefore difficult to detect

B Increases rapidly, just prior to impact

C Is easier to detect if the pilot keeps his/her head and eyes moving

11 The most common cause of sudden incapacitation is:

A A heart attack

B A blood clot

C Acute gastroenteritis

12 Is the decision of a group member usually:

A Better than the average group decision

B The same as the average group decision

C Worse than the average group decision

13 At what time of the day is the body temperature highest?

A 1800

B 1600

C 1500

14 Taking 1 unit of alcohol to equal 1 glass of wine, a woman would reach the approximate 'damage threshold' at:

A 3 glasses per day/14 glasses per week

B 6 glasses per day/25 glasses per week

C 8 glasses per day/30 glasses per week

15 When looking at an object during a night flight, it is best to look:

A slightly to one side of the object

B Away from the object, to catch it in peripheral vision

C Directly at the object

16 In a disorientation situation (e.g. an aerobatic manoeuvre which has gone wrong) which of the following will give the pilot the most reliable guidance:

A The eyes

B The balance sense

C Smell

17 Individuals are more likely to comply with a decision made by someone of:

A Greater age

B Greater status

C Greater education

18 The correct descending order of stressors is:

A Family death, divorce, marriage

B Marriage, divorce, family death

C Divorce, family death, marriage

19 The four flying instruments arranged in the standard 'T' consists of:

A ASI, AH, ALT, DI

B ASI, ALT, VSI, DI

C ASI, AH, ALT, VSI

20 The potentially dangerous condition of hypoglycaemia can effect even healthy individuals, and can be caused by:

A Over-consumption of alcohol

B Sudden reduction in cabin pressure

C Lack of food for many hours, followed by sudden physical exercise or mental anxiety.

1 Following a forced landing in hostile terrain, the survival priorities, in order, are:

A Food, water, location, protection

B Water, location, protection, food

C Protection, location, water, food

2 In NW Europe, winter sea temperatures may be as low as 2°C. A person NOT equipped with an immersion suit or dingy has a life expectancy in such waters of around

A 30 minutes

B 5 hours

C 24 hours

3 The requirements for oxygen at 33,700ft - 40,000ft are:

A Increasing percentage of oxygen in breathing gas

B 100% oxygen

C 100% oxygen under pressure

4 Apparent personality change, impaired judgement, muscular, memory and consciousness impairment, are all symptoms of:

A Hyperventilation

B Anoxia

C Hypoxia

5 Carbon monoxide, produced by smoking, binds to haemoglobin which has .... affinity than oxygen.

A An equal

B A lesser

C A far greater

6 A 2-3 minutes time of useful consciouness equates to an altitude of:

A 25,000ft

B 18,000ft

C 30,000ft

7 A pilot's correct priorities in flight are:

A Assert authority, then fly the aircraft

B Aviate, Navigate, Communicate

C Mirror, signal, manoeuvre

Answer the following 2 questions on the diagram below.

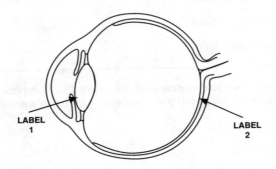

8 Label 1 refers to the ....

A Iris

B Pupil

C Lens

9 Label 2 refers to the ....

A Retina

B Optic Nerve

C Fovea

10 The most toxic of the exhaust gases is?

A Carbon dioxide

B Carbon monoxide

C Cyanide

11 A less experienced co-pilot, believing that the more experienced pilot-in-command has chosen a potentially dangerous course of action should:

A Express openly any doubts

B Try to subtly discuss the subject later

C Say nothing, but adopt the "brace for impact" position

12 A possible antidote for an impulsive attitude is to:

A Take time and think before acting

B Use supplemental oxygen

C Only consider the first option thought of

13 The 'pitch-up' illusion results from:

A An aircraft deceleration

B An aircraft acceleration

C An aircraft vertical movement

14 To reduce stress and increase performance before a cross-country flight, it is best to:

A Allow plenty of time for proper pre-flight planning

B Ignore any adverse factors that might effect the flight

C Eat as little as possible prior to flight

15 The amount of stress on an individual is mainly due to:

A Actual demand and actual ability

B Perceived demand and actual ability

C Perceived demand and perceived ability

16 The comfortable temperature for most people in normal clothing is approximately:

A +15°C

B +30°C

C +20°C

17 The approximate threshold for alcohol intake for men, above which physical damage may be sustained, is taken as:

A 5 units per day/20 units per week

B 10 units per day/50 units per week

C 12 units per day/60 units per week

18 The common symptoms of gastroenteritis include:

A Vomiting, diarrhoea

B Abdominal cramp pains, fever

C All the above

19 Group problem solving will .... the problem solving ability of the ablest member of the group.

A Rarely improve upon

B Improve upon

C Be dramatically worse than

20 The standard instrument 'T' panel is shown below, select the answer which correctly ascertains the instrument layout.

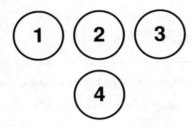

	1	**2**	**3**	**4**
A	ASI	AH	DI	ALT
B	ALT	AH	ASI	DI
C	ASI	AH	ALT	DI

Instructions

1   Time allowed 30 minutes.

2   There are 19 multiple choice questions.

Questions 1 to 18 each carry 5 marks

Question 19 carries 10 marks. For this question ONLY deduct 1 mark for each item missing or in the wrong order. Do not mark this question as less than 0. Your wording need not be exactly that in the given answer, provided the sense and the order is the same. The pass mark is 70 %

3   Read each question carefully as there is only one answer which is correct

4   Remember examination technique. You are advised to pass over questions that seem difficult at first sight and return to them when you have answered the others.

1 The primary reference for an civilian aeronautical RT frequency is:

A An airways flight guide

B AIC's

C The COM section of the AIP

2 A controller is passing you a VDF bearing which is accurate to within 2°, this is classified as class ...

A 1

B A

C 5

3 As height is increased, the range of VHF communications from an aircraft:

A Decreases

B Stays the same

C Increases

4 The RT word that means 'confirm that you have received and understood this message' is:

A Acknowledge

B Affirm

C Confirm

5 The RT word 'climb' means:

A Begin a climb and await further instructions

B Climb, and level-out at any level below that specified

C Climb to and maintain specified level

6 You begin a transmission, and then realise that the radio is set to the wrong frequency. To indicate that the ATSU should ignore the message you should use the word:

A Disregard

B Ignore

C Correction

7 An ATSU wants you to set the code 7000 on your transponder and select mode C. The correct RT phrase would be:

A Monitor 7000, mode C

B Squawk 7000 C

C Send down 7000 with C

8 How would a time of ten to ten (in the morning) be transmitted?

A Ten to Ten Alpha Mike

B Niner Fifty

C Fife Zero or Zero Niner Fife Zero

9 An altimeter setting of 1030 millibars would normally be transmitted as:

A Tree Zero

B Zero Tree Zero

C Wun Zero Tree Zero

10 Which of the following DOES require a read back?

A An instruction to maintain an altitude

B An instruction backtrack a non-active runway

C Surface wind when passed to a landing aircraft

11 An aircraft may abbreviate its call sign:

A When satisfactory two-way communications have been established

B At the pilot's discretion

C Only after the ATSU has abbreviated the aircraft's call sign

12 A 'distress' or 'urgency' call:

A Should initially be made on the frequency in use

B Should only be made on 121.5

C Should be made to the nearest airfield

13 A pilot planning to cross an active MATZ is advised to establish contact

A Only when within the MATZ

B 5 minutes or 15 miles from the MATZ boundary, whichever is greater

C 5 minutes or 15 miles from the airfield, whichever is greater

14 Which of the following best represents station call signs which can be used by an ATC unit?

A control, information, director, ground

B radar, radio, approach, tower

C control, radar, approach, director, tower, ground

15 How might a frequency of 119.725 be written in official documentation?

A 9.725

B 19.725

C 119.72

16 A surface wind of 240/15 could be transmitted as:

A Too Fower Zero degrees Fifteen knots

✓ **B** Too Fower Zero degrees Wun Fife knots

C Too Hundred and Forty Degrees Fifteen knots

---

17 A 'departure' clearance is:

A Clearance to take-off

B Clearance to taxy to the holding point for the active runway

✓ **C** Neither of the above

---

18 When can you change frequency without informing the ATSU you are presently in communication with?

A At the pilot's discretion

B If the ATSU was only giving an FIS or alerting service

✓ **C** Never

---

19 You are a solo student pilot flying a Grumman AA-5 G-DINA 2 miles to the north of Nottingham airfield at 2500 feet on the QNH heading 090° when you experience a complete engine failure. You have Nottingham in sight and you plan to land on runway 27. Detail your radio call (you are already in contact with the air/ground station at Nottingham):

MAYDAY MAYDAY MAYDAY
NOTTINGHAM RADIO
G-DINA GRUMMAN AA-5
TOTAL ENGINE FAILURE
INTEND FORCED LANDING RUNWAY 27 NOTTINGHAM
AIRFIELD.
1 POB.
2 MILES NORTH OF NOTTINGHAM AIRFIELD
2500 FEET QNH ON AIRFIELD QNH
HEADING 090.
AIRFIELD IN SIGHT

1 What type of ATSU can issue clearances?

A Only an ATC unit

B Any ATSU with the call sign 'information'

C Any ATSU that exists at a licensed airfield

2 How would you classify a radio transmission that is readable but with difficulty?

A Readability 3

B Readability 2

C Readability 4

3 The RT word(s) that mean(s) 'I intend to call [unit] on [frequency]' is:

A Changing to...

B Freecall...

C Monitor...

4 Where an ATSU permits a call sign to be abbreviated, the correct abbreviation of Thurston G-ASMY would be:

A Thurston MY

B Thurston GMY

C Thurston G-ASMY

5 The RT word 'descend' means:

A Descend to and maintain the specified level

B Descend to any level above that specified

C Descend, and an instruction to level-out will follow when you reach the cleared level

6 An ATSU instruction to select a transponder code of 7000 could be transmitted as:

A Select Seven Tousand

B Squawk Seven Triple Zero

C Squawk Seven Zero Zero Zero

7 A radio frequency of 119.65 would be transmitted as:

A Wun Nineteen dayseemal Sixty-five

B Wun Nineteen dayseemal Six Fife

C Wun Wun Niner dayseemal Six Fife

8 When a pilot has completed the pre take-off checks and the traffic situation looks suitable, the pilot should report:

A 'Ready for departure'

B 'Ready for take-off'

C 'Ready when you are'

9 An ATSU passes the airfield METAR to an arriving aircraft. The pilot should read back the following information:

A   The complete METAR

B   The altimeter pressure settings

C   No read back is required

10 You are instructed by an ATSU to 'standby'. The correct reply is:

A   'Standing By [call sign]'

B   'Roger standby [then pass message]'

C   No response is expected

11 The correct point to report 'downwind' in the visual circuit is:

A   When abeam the upwind end of the runway in use

B   When abeam the runway mid point

C   When abeam the Aerodrome Reference Point (ARP)

12 What is the correct wording to initiate an urgency message?

A   Urgency, Urgency, Urgency

B   Difficulty message

C   Pan Pan, Pan Pan, Pan Pan

13 When changing the code selected on a transponder:

A   The pilot should always set the transponder to 'standby'

B   The transponder must be switched completely off

C   The transponder can be left set 'on'

14 What type of ATSU uses the call sign 'radio'

A   An ATC unit

B   An AFIS unit at a licensed airfield

C   An air/ground unit

15 A recorded broadcast of an airfield's weather and arrival/departure information is known as an:

A   FIR

B   ATIS

C   AFIB

16 In the visual circuit at a military airfield, the aircraft ahead of you reports 'downwind to roll'. This means it intends to:

A Perform an aerobatic manoeuvre

B Make a touch and go ✓

C Land and exit the runway without stopping

17 Which of the following does NOT need to be included in a Mayday call?

A Aircraft call sign

B Aircraft position

C Pilot's name ✓

18 If making an emergency call on 121.5:

A The pilot MUST address the correct station - London Centre or Scottish Centre

B The pilot should address the call to 'All Stations'

C If in doubt the pilot need not address the call to a specific station

19 You are a student pilot flying solo on a cross country flight from Luton to Shobdon, and you have become completely lost. Your last known position was overhead Banbury at time 15. Your aircraft is G - BNHK, a Cessna 152. Your altitude is 3000 feet on the Cotswold QNH of 1020, heading is 260° and you estimate that you have 1 hour of fuel remaining, the aircraft has a transponder. You are unable to contact the ATSUs on your plan. On what frequency are you going to call for a position fix, and detail the radio message:

121.5
PAN PAN PAN PAN PAN PAN
LONDON CENTRE G-BNHK CESSNA 152
AM COMPLETELY LOST
LAST KNOWN POSITION OVERHEAD BANBURY 15
3000 FEET COTSWOLD QNH 1020 SQUAWKING 7000
HEADING 260
ENDURANCE 1 HOUR

1 A controller passes you a VDF bearing which is accurate to within 5°, this is classified as class ...

A B

B A

C 5

2 The RT word that means 'permission for proposed action is granted' is:

A Acknowledged

B Affirm

C Approved

3 A correct abbreviated call sign for an aircraft with the registration G-DASH would be:

A G-SH

B SH

C G-DA

4 How would a time of 11:25 be transmitted?

A Eleven Twenty-five

B Twenty-five past

C Too Fife or Wun Wun Too Fife

5 An ATSU instruction to climb to and maintain Flight Level 75 could be transmitted as:

A Climb to and maintain Flight Level Seven Fife

B Climb and maintain Flight Level Seven Fife

C Climb Flight Level Seven Fife

6 Runway 06 (magnetic direction 060°) is referred to as:

A Runway six

B Runway six zero

C Runway zero six

7 Which of the following DOES NOT require a read back by the pilot?

A A wind shear warning

B Type of radar service being provided

C A VDF bearing

8 An aircraft has completed its pre take-off checks and checked the traffic situation. Which of the following is the correct request by the pilot for clearance to take-off:

A 'G-RD ready for take-off'

B 'G-BARD ready for departure'

C 'G-RD ready in turn'

9 In the visual circuit, the phrase 'Late Downwind' means:

✓ **A** The aircraft is further along the downwind leg than where a 'downwind' call is normally made

B The aircraft is behind its landing ETA

C Due to an unexpected headwind, the aircraft's ground speed is slower than expected

10 An ATSU instructs you to 'contact [ATSU] on [frequency]'. You should:

A Change to that frequency immediately without making any further transmissions on that frequency

B Transmit your call sign, then change frequency

✓ **C** Make a full read back of the instruction.

11 An aircraft that is in serious and/or imminent danger and requires immediate assistance is in a .... situation:

A Urgency

✓ **B** Distress

C Difficulty

12 An aircraft call sign of Channel 2239 should be transmitted as:

A Channel Twenty-two Thirty-nine

B Too Too Tree Niner

✓ **C** Channel Too Too Tree Niner

13 When receiving a Radar Information Service (RIS):

A The controller will provide traffic information, the pilot decides on what avoiding action to take

B The controller will provide traffic information on any known conflicting traffic and advise on avoiding action

C The controller will provide traffic information of all other aircraft on his radar screen

14 In relation to VDF, a QDM is:

✓ **A** The magnetic track TO the VDF station, e.g. the magnetic heading for the aircraft to steer to reach the VDF station, assuming no wind

B The magnetic track FROM the VDF station, e.g. the magnetic heading for the aircraft to steer to fly away from the VDF station, assuming no wind

C The true track TO the VDF station, e.g. the true heading for the aircraft to steer to reach the VDF station, assuming no wind

15 The spoken abbreviation 'SSR' means:

A Service Stopped - Radar

✓ **B** Secondary Surveillance Radar

C Special Service Requested

16 The FIS service provided by an FIR controller (e.g. call sign London Information):

A Can provide separation from all traffic in the open FIR

B Automatically provides a RIS or RAS

C Can only provide flight details of 'known' traffic ✓

17 An aircraft that reports 'long finals' is:

A More than 4 miles from the runway threshold

B More than 8 miles from the runway threshold

C Between 4 and 8 miles from the runway threshold ✓

18 An aircraft which uses the call sign suffix 'heavy' on initial contact with an ATSU is:

A Having a bad day

B In the ICAO Heavy wake turbulence category ✓

C Operating at or near it's Maximum All Up Weight

19 You are flying a Slingsby G - BNSP, solo, 5 miles west of Finningley at FL 55 heading 110° and talking to Finningley MATZ on 120.35, when the oil pressure falls to zero and the engine begins to run rough - you suspect an engine failure is imminent and you want to divert to Finningley. You are a PPL. Detail your emergency message:

MAYDAY MAYDAY MAYDAY
FINNINGLEY RADAR
G-BNSP SLINGSBY
NIL OIL PRESSURE IMMINENT ENGINE FAILURE
REQUEST IMMEDIATE FORCED LANDING AT FINNINGLEY
5 MILES WEST OF FINNINGLEY
FL 55
HEADING 110
PPL
1 POB

1 The RT word(s) that means 'this is a separation between messages' is:

A Correction

B Break

C New message

2 An ATSU wishes you to climb to and maintain an altitude of 3500 feet. This instruction would be transmitted as:

A Climb to and maintain Tree Tousand Fife Hundred feet

B Climb Tree Fife Zero Zero feet

C Climb to Tree Tousand Fife Hundred feet

3 Where a read back IS NOT required, the phrase to indicate you have understood the message and will co-operate with it is:

A Roger

B Affirm

C Wilco

4 The correct abbreviation of Neatax G-LEAR would be:

A Neatax AR

B Neatax GAR

C No abbreviation is permitted

5 An aircraft gives an ETA of 'Wun Fife'. This time will be:

A 15:00 hours

B 15 minutes from the time of transmission

C 15 minutes past the hour

6 An ATSU instruction to select a transponder code of 2000 could be transmitted as:

A Squawk Too Tousand

B Squawk Twenty Zero Zero

C Squawk Two Zero Zero Zero Zero

7 A radio frequency of 128.50 would be transmitted as:

A Too Ait point Fife Zero

B Too Ait Dayseemal Fife Zero

C Wun Too Ait Dayseemal Fife Zero

8 An ATSU instruction to descend to and maintain Flight Level 50 could be transmitted as:

A Descend to Flight Level Fifty

B Descend Flight Level Fife Zero

C Descend Flight Level Fife Point Zero

9 A controller gives you a VDF bearing which is accurate to within 10°, this is classified as class...

A B

B D

✓ **C** C

---

10 A pilot requests departure information, and is given the runway in use, the surface wind, the number of aircraft in the circuit and the QNH. The pilot should read back:

A Runway in use, surface wind, number of aircraft in the circuit, QNH

✓ **B** Runway in use, QNH

C No read back is required

---

11 A 'departure' clearance is:

✓ **A** The route to be followed after take-off

B Clearance to take-off

C Clearance to enter the departure runway

---

12 An aircraft is inbound to an airfield within controlled airspace. The pilot makes an initial call to the approach frequency and is instructed to 'standby'. The pilot should:

A Orbit at the present position

B Continue into controlled airspace via the flight plan route and await further instructions

✓ **C** Await a further call from the ATSU, but not assume that any clearance has been given

---

13 You make initial contact with an ATSU, request a Radar Advisory Service, and are given a transponder code to 'squawk'. That in itself:

A Means you are receiving a RAS

B Means you are receiving some type of radar-based service

✓ **C** Does not mean you are receiving any form of radar service

---

14 During a cross country flight you become lost and cannot contact any of your planned ATSUs. You decide to call 'Scottish Centre' for assistance, on what frequency?

✓ **A** 121.5

B The ATIS frequency for the nearest major airfield

C The relevant FIS frequency for that part of the FIR

---

15 When can a distress (Mayday) call be simulated between an aircraft and an ATSU?

✓ **A** Never

B Only on 121.5

C If the aircraft uses the words 'Practice Mayday'

16 A pilot can obtain a QDM from:

A Any ATSU

B Any ATC unit

✓ **C** Neither of the above

17 When should an ATSU be open for radio communications?

✓ **A** During the hours of watch notified in the COM section of the AIP

B During the aerodrome's opening hours

C 24 hours a day

18 When flying in class A, B or C airspace, or in class D or E airspace whilst under IFR or at night, a pilot may depart from an Air Traffic Control clearance:

A Never

B Only if the pilot disagrees with it

✓ **C** Only to avoid immediate danger

19 You are downwind in the circuit at Biggin Hill in a Robin DR400 G - BPZP when you suffer a bird strike that shatters the canopy and effects the handling of the aircraft. You decide to make an immediate landing on runway 03. You are at 1000 feet on the QFE, heading 200° and have one passenger - you are a PPL. You are in communication with Biggin Tower and decide to make a distress call. Detail that call:

MAYDAY MAYDAY MAYDAY
BIGGIN TOWER
G-BPZP RUBIN DRAVO
BIRD STRIKE SHATTERED CANOPY AFFECTED HANDLING
INTEND IMMEDIATE FORCED LANDING BIGGIN
                                    RUNWAY 03.

DOWN WIND
1000 FEET BIGGIN QFE
HEADING 200
PPL
2 POB

1 A heading of 220° would be transmitted as:

A   Too Twenty

B   Too Hundred Too Zero

C   Too Too Zero

2 A correct abbreviated call sign for an aircraft with the registration G-BCSL would be:

A   G-SL

B   SL

C   G-BC

3 An ATSU reports that the airfield will close at 'Too Zero'. This time will be:

A   20 minutes past the hour

B   20 minutes to the hour

C   20:00 hours

4 An ATSU wishes you to descend to and maintain a height of 2700 feet. This instruction would be transmitted as:

A   Descend to and maintain Too Tousand Seven Hundred feet

B   Descend to Too Tousand Seven Hundred feet

C   Descend Too Tousand Seven Hundred feet

5 Runway 24 (magnetic direction 240°) is referred to as:

A   Runway twenty-four

B   Runway Too Forty

C   Runway Too Fower

6 Which of the following most accurately represents items that MUST be read-back by a pilot?

A   Speed instructions, clearance to backtrack an active runway, a frequency change instigated by the pilot, runway in use

B   Heading instructions, a VDF bearing, type of radar service being offered, range and bearing of conflicting traffic, route clearance

C   Altimeter settings, level instructions, a METAR, clearance to cross an active runway, an SSR code

7 When an aircraft's transponder is set to 'Standby' or 'SBY':

A   On the controllers radar screen the abbreviation 'SBY' appears next to the aircraft's primary return

B   On the controllers radar screen the code selected is 'frozen', until the next code is selected

C   No secondary return is seen on the controllers screen

8 The Morse code ... --- ... (SOS) indicates:

A An urgency (Pan) situation

B A difficulty situation

✓ **C** A distress (Mayday) situation

9 Upon hearing a Mayday call, all other aircraft on the frequency:

A Must maintain radio silence under all circumstances

✓ **B** Can break radio silence if they can offer assistance to the aircraft in distress

C Can only break radio silence if authorised to do so by the ATSU

10 How would you classify a radio transmission that is unreadable ?

✓ **A** Readability 1

B Readability 0

C Readability 4

11 What is the CAA recommended maximum height/range for establishing two-way communications with a small airfield:

A 3 miles and 1000 feet

✓ **B** 10 miles and 3000 feet

C 100 miles and 30000 feet

12 The spoken abbreviation 'DF' means:

A Dedicated Frequency

✓ **B** Direction Finding

C Delay Flight

13 Which of the following is true of a Radar Advisory Service (RAS)?

A The pilot MUST comply with the avoiding action passed by the controller

✓ **B** The pilot can decide not to take the controllers advice on avoiding action, but in this case he must inform the controller and the pilot becomes responsible for taking avoiding action

C The pilot can decide not to take the controllers advice on avoiding action, without needing to inform the controller

14 During a cross country flight you become lost and cannot contact any of your planned ATSUs. You decide to call 'London Centre' for assistance - on what frequency?

A The relevant FIS frequency for that part of the FIR

B The ATIS frequency for the nearest major airfield

✓ **C** 121.5

15 During a visual go-around, and unless there are specific instructions otherwise, you would normally climb:

✓ **A** To the 'dead' side of the runway

B To the 'live' side of the runway

C Straight ahead directly over the runway

16 What is the correct wording to initiate a distress message ?

A Distress, Distress, Distress

B Emergency call

✓ **C** Mayday, Mayday, Mayday

17 An aircraft is instructed by ATC to 'expedite' a descent. This means the pilot should:

A Increase the aircraft's airspeed

✓ **B** Increase the aircraft's rate of descent

C Reduce the current rate of descent

18 'London Volmet South' broadcasts:

A The current TAFs (forecasts) for selected airfields

✓ **B** The current METARS (actuals) for selected airfields

C Neither of the above

19 You are a PPL flying with one passenger in a Piper Malibu aircraft with a call sign of Autoair 03. You suffer a complete engine failure when 1 mile north of Lymington, altitude 1500 feet. Your heading is 340° and you are talking to Southampton approach on 128.85. You intend to make a forced landing at Beaulieu disused airfield. Write out the correct distress call.

MAYDAY MAYDAY MAYDAY
SOUTHAMPTON APPROACH
AUTOAIR 03   PIPER MALIBU
TOTAL ENGINE FAILURE
INTEND FORCED LANDING AT BEAULIEU DISUSED A/F
1 MILE NORTH OF LYMINGTON
1500 FEET
HEADING 340
PPL
2 POB

1 An altimeter subscale setting of 1014 millibars would be transmitted as:

A Ten Fourteen

B Wun Tousand and Fourteen

C Wun Zero Wun Fower

2 How would you classify a radio transmission that is readable now and then ?

A Readability 3

B Readability 2

C Readability 4

3 If an ATSU wishes to instruct you to call another ATSU that already has your details, they will use the word/phrase:

A Contact

B Change to

C Freecall

4 The correct abbreviation of Speedbird 5536 would be:

A Speedbird 36

B No abbreviation is permitted

C 5536

5 An ATSU instruction to descend to and maintain an altitude of 1800 feet would be spoken as:

A Descend to and maintain Wun Tousand Ait Hundred feet

B Descend to Eighteen Hundred feet

C Descend to Wun Tousand Ait Hundred feet

6 A heading of 140° would be transmitted as:

A Fower Zero

B Wun Hundred and Forty

C Wun Fower Zero

7 When an ATC unit has acknowledged correct read back of a departure clearance:

A The aircraft still requires a separate take-off clearance

B The aircraft can take-off in turn

C The aircraft can take-off when ready

8 An ATSU passes the following arrival information to an inbound aircraft:

'Runway in use 24, surface wind 300 degrees 5 knots, visibility 15 kilometres, weather nil. Cloud scattered at 2500. Temperature +15, dewpoint +8. QNH 1025, QFE for 24 1015.'

Given a call sign of Raven 09, how would this information be read back?

A 'Roger the weather Raven 09'

B 'Copy the weather Raven 09'

C 'Runway 24, QNH 1025, QFE 1015 Raven 09'

9 During a flight over inhospitable terrain you spot an aircraft that has made a successful forced landing, with survivors requiring assistance. You should:

A Make a Mayday call on the frequency in use

B Make a Pan call on the frequency in use

C Change to 121.5 and make a Pan call

10 A controller reports to you that the ATSU has 'negative SSR'. This means that:

A The controller is receiving a negative value transponder code

B You should turn-off your transponder

C The ATSU is not equipped to receive an transponder code

11 A transponder without 'altitude read-out' capability is described as:

A Mode A

B Four figure only

C Cheap

12 What type of ATSU has the call sign 'tower'

A An ATC Unit

B An AFIS Unit or an ATC Unit

C An AFIS unit in a control tower

13 An ATSU wishes to broadcast a message to all aircraft on the frequency. It will preface its broadcast with '.............'and such a message .... generally require a read back:

A 'General broadcast'; does not

B 'All aircraft on frequency'; does

C 'All stations'; does not

14 The abbreviation FIS means:

A Final Instruction Sent

B First Initiate Standby

C Flight Information Service

15 When receiving a Radar Advisory Service (RAS):

A The controller will pass information on any known conflicting traffic and advise on avoiding action

B The controller will pass information on any known conflicting traffic, the pilot decides what avoiding action is necessary

C The controller will pass information on conflicting traffic the pilot spots

16 You are in the visual circuit at an airfield inside controlled airspace, when your radio fails. You should:

A Vacate controlled airspace immediately and land at a 'non-radio' airfield

B Continue in accordance with the last ATSU instruction, looking for light signals from the ATSU

C Fly a left-hand triangle and await a 'shepherd' aircraft

17 An aircraft broadcasts a 'Mayday' call on the frequency you are using, but the ATSU does not reply. You should:

A Maintain radio silence

B Tell the 'Mayday' aircraft to 'say again'

C Relay the 'Mayday' call to the ATSU

18 You fly regularly to an airfield, which usually has a call sign '[ATSU name] information'. One day the call sign is '[ATSU name] radio'. This means that:

A The airfield is now unlicensed

B A trainee radio operator is using the radio under supervision

C Only an air/ground radio service is available

19 You are in a Piper Arrow G-BNZG flying across the English Channel to the Channel Islands when you spot a small boat in difficulties 10 miles south of the Isle of Wight. You are at 3000 feet and begin a right-hand orbit to keep the boat in sight while you fix the exact position. You are talking to London Information, and you want to request Coastguard assistance. You are a PPL with an IMC rating:

MAYDAY MAYDAY MAYDAY
LONDON INFORMATION
G-BNZG PIPER ARROW
HAS SPOTTED SMALL BOAT IN DIFFICULTY
10 MILES SOUTH OF THE ISLE OF WIGHT
G-BNZG IS ORBITING THE BOAT
AT 3000 FEET PPL WITH IMC
REQUEST COASTGUARD ASSISTANCE

1 How would you classify a radio transmission that is perfectly readable?

A Readability 1

B Readability 5

C Readability A

2 An ATSU makes an error in a transmission. To indicate an error has occurred, and preface the proper version, they will use the word/phrase:

A Correction

B Say again

C Disregard

3 You did not receive properly an ATSU transmission to you. You should:

A Request them to 'say again'

B Request them to 'repeat'

C Request them to 'speak up a bit'

4 An ATSU instruction to maintain a height of 1200 feet would be transmitted as:

A Maintain Twelve Hundred feet

B Maintain Wun Too Zero Zero feet

C Maintain Wun Tousand Too Hundred feet

5 An altimeter setting of 995 millibars would be transmitted as

A Niner Niner Fife

B Niner Ninety-five

C Niner Niner Fife millibars

6 Which of the following most accurately represents items that must be read back by a pilot?

A A departure clearance, clearance to continuing holding short of an active runway, an instruction to 'recycle' a transponder code, any message when a read back is requested by ATC

B An altimeter setting, clearance to land, a frequency change, runway in use, a descent instruction, a met report of an active Cumulonimbus

C Any level instruction, an airways clearance (when it is the same as flight plan), a QFE, a QDM, a visibility report if it is below 1000 metres.

7 The pilot of an aircraft with the call sign of G-ER has requested departure information, and in reply is given 'Runway in use 15, surface wind 170/10, QNH 1015'. What would be the correct read back?

A 'Runway in use 15, surface wind 170/10, QNH 1015 G-ER'

B 'Runway 15, QNH 1015 G-ER'

C 'Roger the information, G-ER'

8 A radio frequency of 128.175 would be transmitted as:

A Wun Too Ait dayseemal Wun Seven Fife

B Wun Too Ait Wun Seven Fife

C Wun Too Ait dayseemal Wun Seven

9 It is not your day. You are making a Pan call, when your conversation is interrupted by a Mayday call. You should:

A Continue your conversation over the Mayday call

B Resume your Pan conversation as soon as the Mayday transmission ends

C Maintain silence whilst the Mayday is in progress

10 You are at the holding point for the active runway, and in reply to your request for departure ATC reply 'cleared immediate take-off'. You may:

A Taxy onto the runway immediately and commence take-off without stopping

B Reply 'Unable comply' and hold position

C Either of the above, at the pilot's option

11 You have established two-way communication on a frequency of 119.65, when you experience an emergency that necessitates a 'Mayday' call. On what frequency should the call be made?

A 121.5

B 119.65

C The next planned frequency

12 When receiving a Radar Advisory Service (RAS) or a Radar Information Service (RIS), which of the following is true:

A The controller and the pilot are jointly responsible for terrain separation

B The controller is solely responsible for terrain separation

C The pilot is wholly responsible for terrain separation

13 The phrase 'unknown traffic' used by a controller means:

A Traffic whose call sign is unknown

B Traffic whose flight details are not known to that particular ATSU

C Non-radio traffic

14 In response to the instruction 'contact Liverpool approach on 119.85', the correct acknowledgement would be:

A 'Wilco [call sign]'

B 'Roger, changing frequency'

C 'Liverpool Approach 119.85 [call sign]'

15 When requesting a QDM to reach an airfield:

A The pilot must request regular QDMs to confirm the correct track is being followed

B The QDM will not change once it has been given

C The pilot must calculate further QDMs unaided

16 If the PTT (Press To Transmit) button on an aircraft becomes stuck 'open'

A The transmitter becomes U/S

B Everything said on the intercom is broadcast

C The PTT cannot become stuck in the 'transmit' position

17 In the 'speechless' code, one short 'dot' transmitted by an aircraft means:

A Yes or acknowledged

B No

C Say again

18 Which of the following may not be practised on 121.5?

A An urgency situation (Pan)

B A distress situation (Mayday)

C Both A & B

19 You hear a Mayday call from G-BNCR, a Piper Warrior with an engine fire, 4 miles south of Thame at altitude 2000 feet heading 270°. The pilot, a CPL is flying solo and intends to make an immediate forced landing. If the ATSU (Wycombe tower) does not hear the call, how would you relay it (your call sign is G-BXPS)?

MAYDAY   MAYDAY   MAYDAY
WYCOMBE TOWER
G-BXPS HAS INTERCEPTED A MAYDAY CALL FROM G-BNCR
I SAY AGAIN
G-BNCR PIPER WARRIOR WITH ENGINE FIRE
4 MILES SOUTH OF THAME
AT 2000 FEET
HEADING 270°
PILOT CPL INTENDS IMMEDIATE FORCED LANDING
1 POB

1 What exactly is the aviation VHF frequency 'WUN WUN AIT DAYSEEMAL SIX TOO'?

A 118.60

B 1186.25

C 118.625 ✓

2 A controller is passing you a VDF bearing whose accuracy is worse than 10° , this is classified as class ...

A Unclassified

B D ✓

C C

3 To indicate that your message is ended, and you do expect a reply, you can use the word:

A Over ✓

B Out

C Reply

4 In the UK, to request a station to proceed in giving their flight details the correct phrase is:

A Go ahead

B Pass your message ✓

C Pass your details

5 An ATSU instruction to descend to and maintain Flight Level 110 could be transmitted as:

A Descend Flight Level Wun Ten

B Descend Flight Level Eleven

C Descend Flight Level Wun Wun Zero ✓

6 After reporting established on finals, you are instructed by an ATSU to 'Continue approach'. This means:

A You are cleared to land

B Continue the approach, you are not yet cleared to land ✓

C You are cleared to go-around

7 The established visual circuit is left-hand on runway 26. You make a visual go-around after approaching 26, during the climb you should:

A Route directly over runway 26

B Turn left to fly to the left of runway 26

C Turn right to fly to the right of runway 26 ✓

8 The ATSU call sign 'Director' signifies:

A An approach control radar service

B The radio operator is a senior airfield manager

C A non-radar en-route navigation service

9 An AFIS unit (call sign Bogborough Information) passes you the following message:

"Unofficial observation from Bogborough gives the cloud base as 600 feet". This means:

A The cloud base has been estimated visually

B The cloud base has been estimated by a non-accredited person

C The cloud base is changeable

10 An aircraft ahead of you in the visual circuit announced the intention to make a 'full stop'. You can expect it will:

A Land and stop on the runway

B Land, stop on the runway, wait for not more than 2 minutes then take-off again

C Land and vacate the runway (as opposed to making a touch and go)

11 You are holding, waiting to make an approach to an airfield. If your fuel situation becomes critical you should:

A Make a 'fuel critical' message to receive priority over other traffic

B Request 'fuel emergency' status to receive priority over other traffic

C Make a Distress or Urgency message as appropriate. Without declaring an emergency you will not receive priority over other traffic

12 You are flying VFR outside controlled airspace, and have not been allocated a transponder code by an ATSU:

A You may squawk 7000

B You may not use a squawk without ATC instructions .

C You may squawk 4321

13 An aircraft cleared to line-up on the runway requests a 'backtrack'. This means it wants to:

A Reverse up the runway

B Take-off in the opposite direction to that indicated

C Taxy up the runway in the reverse direction to landing direction

14 The RT phrase 'Squawk standby' means:

A Set the transponder to the standby position

B Standby for a new squawk code, continue squawking the existing code

C Squawk the conspicuity code

15 A controller reports to you 'not receiving mode Charlie'. This means:

A Your altimeter subscale is incorrectly set

B The controller cannot see the aircraft's 'secondary' return

✓ **C** The controller cannot see any height read-out from the aircraft's transponder

16 A controller giving you a radar service describes a conflicting aircraft as 'unknown traffic'. This means:

✓ **A** The ATSU does not know the traffic's flight details

B The traffic is not in contact with any ATSU

C The traffic is a UFO

17 A distress call on 121.5 when an aircraft is north of 55° N would normally be answered by:

✓ **A** 'Scottish centre'

B The nearest ATSU

C 'UK centre'

18 You are holding at a holding point some way down the runway. In order to taxy up to the threshold to make full use of the available runway length for take-off you should request:

A 'full length take-off'

B 'Backtrack'

C 'Threshold departure'

19 You are flying 1 mile west of Clevedon at FL50 heading 160°, in a Rockwell Commander, G-DASH when the engine begins to run rough. You decide to divert to Bristol airfield, whose approach service you are already talking to. You are a PPL with 2 passengers. Write out the correct urgency call:

PAN PAN PAN PAN PAN PAN
BRISTOL APPROACH
G-DASH ROCKWELL COMMANDER
ENGINE RUNNING ROUGH
REQUEST URGENT DIVERSION TO BRISTOL AIRFIELD
1 MILE WEST OF CLEVEDON
FL 50
HEADING 160
PPL 3 POB.

1 An ATSU instruction to climb to and maintain Flight Level 45 could be transmitted as:

A Climb to Flight Level Forty-five

B Climb Flight Level Fower point Fife

C Climb Flight Level Fower Fife

---

2 How would you classify a radio transmission that is readable?

A Readability 3

B Readability 2

C Readability 4

---

3 To indicate 'no; OR that is not correct; OR permission is not granted' the correct RT word is:

A Negatory

B Negative

C Nullify

---

4 The correct abbreviation of Britannia 716 would be:

A Britannia 16

B 716

C Neither of the above

---

5 How would a time of 14:47 be transmitted?

A Fourteen Forty-seven or Forty-seven

B Too Forty-seven

C Fower Seven

---

6 What is the meaning of the phrase 'unable comply'?

A I cannot carry out that instruction

B I do not understand that instruction

C I did not hear that instruction

---

7 A cloud base of 2800 feet would be transmitted as:

A Twenty Ait Zero Zero feet

B Too dayseemal Ait Tousand feet

C Too Tousand Ait Hundred feet

---

8 When should a pilot use the phrase 'take-off'?

A Never

B To request clearance to take-off

C Only after the ATSU has given take-off clearance

9 You are unable to establish proper two-way communications with an ATSU, but the receiver is working and you believe the transmitter is still transmitting 'carrier wave'. In the speechless code, to request a 'homing' (e.g. QDM) you should:

A Transmit one long 'dash' (2 seconds): __

B Transmit one short 'dot': .

C Transmit four short 'dots': ....

10 What is the transponder code to indicate that the aircraft has suffered a radio failure?

A 7700

B 7600

C 6000

11 The 'Volume' control on an aircraft radio:

A Can be turned down sufficiently so that other radio transmissions cannot be heard

B Is designed so that it cannot be turned down sufficiently to lose radio contact

C Also controls the transmitter volume

12 In the 'speechless' code, to indicate 'say again' the pilot should transmit:

A Three 'dots': ...

B The Morse letter X : -..-

C The Morse letters SA: ... .-

13 At an airfield with an ATC unit, you accept a 'land after' clearance (there is one aircraft already on the runway, taxying to the end to vacate). Who is responsible for maintaining separation between the aircraft?

A The controller

B You, as the pilot of the following aircraft

C Neither of the above

14 After reporting 'downwind' you are receive the instruction 'cleared to final number 1'. This means:

A You are number one in the landing sequence

B No other aircraft will take-off or land before you

C You are the only aircraft in the circuit

15 Flying on a Sunday, you receive no reply after three consecutive calls on a MATZ frequency. You can assume:

A You have suffered a radio failure

B The ATSU is closed, you may fly through the airfield's ATZ

C The ATSU is closed, you may not fly through the airfield's ATZ

16 What would be the correct read back be of the following arrival information, by the pilot of an aircraft with the call sign G-VU:

'Runway 16, surface wind 130/15, QNH 1014 QFE 1009, four in the circuit'

A 'Runway 16, surface wind 130/15, QNH 1014 QFE 1009, four in the circuit G-VU'

✓ **B** 'Runway 16, QNH 1014, QFE 1009 G-VU'

C 'Runway 16, QNH 1014, QFE 1009, traffic copied'

17 You are receiving an FIS service from an FIR controller on a very busy frequency. When you wish to change frequency:

A You can do so without calling the controller

B You can do so without calling the ATSU provided you contact them by telephone after landing

✓ **C** You must inform the controller

18 You hear a 'Mayday' being broadcast. Your initial action should be:

✓ **A** Write down details of the Mayday, maintain radio silence and be ready to offer assistance if you can

B After the ATSU has acknowledged the Mayday, do so also

C Instruct the 'Mayday' aircraft to change frequency to 121.5

19 Your aircraft is a Cessna 172 registration G - BFLV, flying 4 miles south west of Chester on a heading of 270 at an altitude of 2000 feet. You are a PPL and have 3 passengers, one of whom has a suspected heart attack. You decide to divert directly to Liverpool (which you have in sight). You are already in contact with Liverpool approach, detail the radio call:

~~MAYDAY MAYDAY~~ MAYDAY PAN
LIVERPOOL APPROACH
G-BFLV CESSNA 172
PASSENGER WITH SUSPECTED HEART ATTACK
REQUEST ~~INTEND~~ IMMEDIATE DIVERSION TO LIVERPOOL
4 MILES S.W OF CHESTER
2000 FEET
HDG 270
PPL 3 POB
AT INSIGUT

AND AMBULANCE ON ARRIVAL

1 An aircraft makes contact with an ATSU at time 14:17, and has ten minutes to go before reaching the airfield overhead. It should give its ETA for overhead the airfield as:

A Twenty-seven

B Wun Zero

C Too Seven

2 An ATSU instruction to maintain altitude 2200 feet would be transmitted as:

A Maintain Flight Level 2.2

B Maintain Too Tousand Too Hundred feet

C Maintain Twenty-two Hundred feet

3 After landing, a 'runway vacated' call can be made by the pilot:

A When the aircraft reaches the end of the runway

B As the aircraft turns to backtrack the runway

C Once the aircraft clears (passes the holding point of) the runway

4 An ATSU instruction to climb to and maintain Flight Level 120 could be transmitted as:

A Climb Flight Level Wun Too Zero

B Climb Flight Level Twelve

C Climb Flight Level Wun Twenty

5 A cloud base of 1400 feet would be transmitted as:

A Fourteen Hundred feet

B Wun Tousand Fower Hundred feet

C Wun Fower Zero Zero feet

6 When can a pilot tell an ATSU to 'standby'?

A Never

B Only in an urgency or distress situation

C At any time

7 You have experienced a radio receiver failure, but believe the transmitter is still working. You should make standard position reports preceded by:

A '[Call sign] transmitting blind...'

B '[Call sign] all station...'

C '[Call sign] general broadcast...'

8 The transponder code 7700:

A   Can only be selected on ATC instructions

B   Can be used to simulate an emergency, as long as you have broadcast this intention to the ATSU

C   Should only be used in a genuine emergency

9 In an emergency situation, who can impose radio silence on all other aircraft?

A   The ATSU

B   The aircraft in difficulties

C   Both A & B

10 An aircraft has a very urgent message concerning the safety of an aircraft or some person in it, or some person or vehicle in sight of the aircraft. This is a .... situation:

A   Urgency

B   Difficulty

C   Distress

11 The Morse code -..- -..- -..- (XXX) indicates:

A   A distress (Mayday) situation

B   An urgency (Pan) situation

C   A homing required in the speechless code

12 What type of ATSU has the call sign 'information'

A   An ATSU providing a service in the 'open FIR'

B   An AFIS Unit

C   An AFIS or air/ground unit

13 Having contacted a VDF station, you are receiving a series of QDMs. Which of the following is correct for an aircraft's request for a further QDM?

A   'Request QDM, G-FE over'

B   'G-FE request DF'

C   'What is my QDM?'

14 Which of the following is true of a Radar Information Service (RIS)?

A   The controller and the pilot are jointly responsible for traffic separation

B   The controller is solely responsible for traffic separation

C   The pilot is wholly responsible for separation from other aircraft, whether or not the controller has given traffic information

15 A military controller may use the phrase 'wait' which:

A   Means orbit in your present position

✓ B   Has the same meaning as 'standby'

C   Means call again in 30 seconds

16 When will a 'land after' clearance NOT be given to a pilot?

A   When the following aircraft is bigger than the leading aircraft

B   When the following aircraft has a faster approach speed than the leading aircraft

✓ C   At night

17 You receive the clearance 'G-UD cleared to land 19, surface wind 190/15'. The correct read back is:

✓ A   'Cleared to land 19 G-UD'

B   'Cleared to land 19, 190/15'

C   'Cleared to land 19'

18 An aircraft with the call sign Monarch 874 may abbreviate that call sign:

A   Once an ATSU has done so

B   Once satisfactory two-way communications are established

C   Never

19 You are the PPL pilot of a TB 10 Tobago call sign G-BKIS, flying from Birmingham to East Midlands with 2 passengers. As you pass 3 miles east abeam Sutton Coldfield you discover a problem in the fuel system meaning that you can only select a tank with an estimated 30 minutes fuel remaining. You decide to return to Birmingham and start a left-hand turn to do so. You are at altitude 2500 feet and currently talking to Birmingham Approach. Detail the correct emergency message:

~~MAYDAY MAYDAY MAYDAY~~ PAN

BIRMINGHAM APPROACH

G-BKIS TB10 TOBAGO

RUNNING SHORT OF FUEL

INTEND EMERGENCY LANDING AT BIRMINGHAM

3 MILES EAST ABEAM SUTTON COLDFIELD

2500 FEET

TURNING BACK TO BIRMINGHAM

PPL 3 POB

ESTIMATE 30 MIN FUEL ENDURANCE

Aviation Law
Meteorology
Navigation
Human Performance and Limitations
Radiotelephony

20 Questions @ 5 marks each
(RT 18 Questions @ 5 marks each, question 19 - 10 marks)

Correctly answered Questions	Mark %	
1	5	
2	10	
3	15	
4	20	
5	25	
6	30	
7	35	
8	40	
9	45	
10	50	
11	55	
12	60	
13	65	FAIL
14	70	**PASS**
15	75	
16	80	
17	85	
18	90	
19	95	
20	100	

Aircraft General

50 Questions @ 2 marks each

Correctly answered Questions	Mark %		Correctly answered Questions	Mark %	
1	2		26	52	
2	4		27	54	
3	6		28	56	
4	8		29	58	
5	10		30	60	
6	12		31	62	
7	14		32	64	
8	16		33	66	
9	18		34	68	FAIL
10	20				
11	22		**35**	**70**	**PASS**
12	24		**36**	**72**	
13	26		**37**	**74**	
14	28		**38**	**76**	
15	30		**39**	**78**	
16	32		**40**	**80**	
17	34		**41**	**82**	
18	36		**42**	**84**	
19	38		**43**	**86**	
20	40		**44**	**88**	
21	42		**45**	**90**	
22	44		**46**	**92**	
23	46		**47**	**94**	
24	48		**48**	**96**	
25	50		**49**	**98**	
			50	**100**	

PAPER 1

1	C	11	A
2	C	12	A
3	A	13	A
4	B	14	A
5	A	15	C
6	B	16	C
7	C	17	C
8	B	18	B
9	C	19	C
10	B	20	C

PAPER 2

5	B	15	B
6	C	16	C
7	A	17	A
8	C	18	A
9	C	19	A
10	B	20	B

PAPER 3

5	A	15	C
6	C	16	B
7	B	17	A
8	C	18	B
9	A	19	A
10	B	20	C

PAPER 4

1	C	11	B
2	C	12	C
3	B	13	A
4	B	14	C
5	B	15	B
6	B	16	B
7	A	17	B
8	B	18	A
9	C	19	C
10	C	20	C

PAPER 5

1	A	11	B
2	A	12	B
3	A	13	B
4	A	14	B
5	C	15	C
6	C	16	A
7	B	17	B
8	B	18	C
9	C	19	A
10	C	20	A

PAPER 6

1	B	11	C
2	B	12	B
3	C	13	C
4	A	14	C
5	B	15	B
6	B	16	B
7	B	17	B
8	C	18	C
9	A	19	B
10	B	20	A

PAPER 7

1	B	11	A
2	A	12	A
3	A	13	B
4	C	14	B
5	C	15	A
6	C	16	A
7	B	17	B
8	C	18	C
9	A	19	B
10	C	20	A

PAPER 8

1	A	11	A
2	C	12	A
3	A	13	C
4	A	14	C
5	A	15	C
6	B	16	A
7	B	17	C
8	B	18	C
9	C	19	B
10	C	20	C

PAPER 9

1	B	11	A
2	B	12	C
3	B	13	B
4	A	14	A
5	A	15	B
6	A	16	C
7	B	17	C
8	A	18	C
9	B	19	B
10	A	20	C

PAPER 10

1	B	11	C
2	B	12	C
3	C	13	B
4	C	14	B
5	C	15	A
6	B	16	A
7	A	17	A
8	B	18	A
9	B	19	C
10	A	20	B

PAPER 1

1 A	11 C
2 C	12 B
3 B	13 A
4 C	14 C
5 A	15 A
6 B	16 B
7 A	17 C
8 C	18 A
9 B	19 B
10 C	20 B

PAPER 2

1 B	11 C
2 A	12 A
3 A	13 B
4 C	14 B
5 B	15 A
6 C	16 C
7 A	17 C
8 C	18 B
9 B	19 C
10 C	20 C

PAPER 3

1 B	11 B
2 C	12 A
3 A	13 C
4 A	14 A
5 C	15 A
6 B	16 A
7 A	17 C
8 B	18 C
9 C	19 C
10 C	20 B

PAPER 4

1 C	11 B
2 A	12 B
3 B	13 A
4 A	14 B
5 C	15 C
6 B	16 C
7 B	17 A
8 A	18 B
9 C	19 C
10 A	20 A

PAPER 5

1 C	11 C
2 B	12 A
3 B	13 A
4 A	14 B
5 C	15 C
6 A	16 B
7 B	17 B
8 C	18 C
9 A	19 B
10 A	20 C

PAPER 6

1 B	11 A
2 B	12 C
3 A	13 B
4 B	14 B
5 C	15 C
6 A	16 C
7 C	17 A
8 B	18 C
9 C	19 C
10 A	20 A

PAPER 7

1 A	11 B
2 B	12 B
3 A	13 A
4 A	14 A
5 B	15 A
6 A	16 B
7 A	17 B
8 B	18 C
9 B	19 C
10 B	20 A

PAPER 8

1 C	11 B
2 A	12 B
3 C	13 A
4 B	14 B
5 A	15 C
6 B	16 A
7 C	17 B
8 A	18 C
9 A	19 A
10 C	20 C

PAPER 9

1 B	11 A
2 C	12 C
3 C	13 B
4 B	14 C
5 A	15 C
6 B	16 A
7 C	17 B
8 B	18 C
9 B	19 B
10 A	20 B

PAPER 10

1 C	11 B
2 B	12 A
3 C	13 A
4 B	14 A
5 A	15 C
6 B	16 B
7 C	17 A
8 C	18 B
9 A	19 C
10 C	20 A

PAPER 1

1	B	11	C
2	C	12	B
3	B	13	B
4	C	14	A
5	C	15	C
6	C	16	B
7	A	17	C
8	B	18	A
9	B	19	B
10	A	20	A

PAPER 2

1	A	11	A
2	B	12	C
3	A	13	A
4	C	14	C
5	C	15	B
6	C	16	C
7	A	17	A
8	B	18	A
9	B	19	A
10	A	20	C

PAPER 3

1	B	11	C
2	B	12	A
3	B	13	C
4	A	14	C
5	A	15	B
6	A	16	C
7	B	17	A
8	C	18	A
9	B	19	B
10	B	20	A

PAPER 4

1	A	11	B
2	C	12	A
3	C	13	C
4	A	14	C
5	B	15	B
6	A	16	C
7	A	17	B
8	B	18	A
9	C	19	A
10	B	20	C

PAPER 5

1	A	11	A
2	C	12	B
3	B	13	A
4	B	14	C
5	C	15	A
6	C	16	B
7	A	17	B
8	B	18	C
9	C	19	B
10	B	20	B

PAPER 6

1	A	11	B
2	C	12	C
3	A	13	B
4	B	14	C
5	B	15	A
6	C	16	C
7	B	17	A
8	B	18	C
9	A	19	B
10	A	20	A

PAPER 7

1	B	11	A
2	A	12	C
3	B	13	A
4	B	14	C
5	C	15	B
6	A	16	B
7	A	17	A
8	B	18	B
9	A	19	C
10	A	20	B

PAPER 8

1	B	11	C
2	A	12	C
3	C	13	A
4	C	14	C
5	B	15	B
6	C	16	C
7	C	17	A
8	B	18	C
9	A	19	C
10	B	20	A

PAPER 9

1	B	11	C
2	C	12	A
3	A	13	B
4	C	14	A
5	C	15	C
6	B	16	C
7	A	17	B
8	B	18	B
9	C	19	C
10	A	20	A

PAPER 10

1	B	11	B
2	A	12	A
3	B	13	C
4	B	14	C
5	C	15	B
6	A	16	B
7	C	17	A
8	A	18	A
9	B	19	C
10	C	20	B

From	To	FL/Alt ft amsl	Safety Alt	Tas kt	W/V	Trk T	Drift	Hdg T	Var	Hdg M	GS kt	Dist nm	Time hr/min
Goodwood	Grove	3000	**2300**	85	250/20	**330**	**12°S**	**318**	**4.5W**	**332.5**	**80**	**51**	**38**
Goodwood	Shobdon	3500	**2800**	85	270/15	**306**	**6°S**	**300**	**5W**	**305**	**72**	**66**	**55**
										Total		**117**	**93**

From	To	FL/Alt	Safety Alt ft amsl	Tas kt	W/V	.Trk T	Drift	Hdg T	Var	Hdg M	GS kt	Dist nm	Time hr/min
Shoreham	Canterbury	2,000	2100	85	175/15	061	9°P	070	4°W	074	90	56	37
Canterbury	Stapleford	2,000	1900	85	190/20	304	8°S	292	4°W	296	91	38	25
										Total	94	62

From	To	FL/Alt	Safety Alt ft amsl	Tas kt	W/V	Trk T	Drift	Hdg T	Var	Hdg M	GS kt	Dist nm	Time hr/min
Hucknall (53°00'N) (01°13'W)	Hawarden	3,000	3200	85	260/15	279	3°S	276	5W	281	71	64	54
Hawarden	Manchester (53°21'N) (02°16'W)	2,000	1800	90	280/20	067	7°S	060	5W	065	106	27	15
										Total	91	69

From	To	FL/Alt ft amsl	Safety Alt ft amsl	Tas kt	W/V	Trk T	Drift	Hdg T	Var	Hdg M	GS kt	Dist nm	Time hr/min
Skegness (53°11'N) (00°20'E)	Hucknall (53°00'N) (01°13'W)	2,000	1900	85	010/20	260	13°P	273	5W	278	89	57	38.5
Hucknall	Netherthorpe (53°19'N) (01°11'W)	2,000	2100	85	350/15	003	2°S	001	5W	006	69	18	15.5
											Total	75	54

From	To	FL/Alt	Safety Alt ft amsl	Tas kt	W/V	Trk T	Drift	Hdg T	Var	Hdg M	GS kt	Dist nm	Time hr/min
Bournemouth (50°46'N) (01°50'W)	Dunkeswell (50°51'N) (03°13'W)	2,000	**2600**	90	220/20	**275**	10°S	265	5W	**270**	**77**	**53**	**41.5**
Dunkeswell	Bristol (51°25'N) (02°42'W)	1,500	**3000**	95	260/25	**031**	13°S	018	5W	**023**	**109**	**37**	**20.5**
										Total		**90**	**62**

From	To	FL/Alt	Safety Alt ft amsl	Tas kt	W/V	Trk T	Drift	Hdg T	Var	Hdg M	GS kt	Dist nm	Time hr/min
Gloucester Staverton (51°23'N) (02°10'W)	Northampton Sywell (52°18'N) (00°48'W)	3,000	2200	92	190/22	064	12°P	076	5W	081	103	56	32.5
Northampton Sywell	Cambridge (52°12'N) (00°11'E)	2,000	2000	90	180/18	099	11°P	110	5W	115	85	36	25.5
										Total	92	58

From	To	FL/Alt	Safety Alt ft amsl	Tas kt	W/V	Trk T	Drift	Hdg T	Var	Hdg M	GS kt	Dist nm	Time hr/min
Bembridge I.O.W. (50°41'N) (01°06'W)	Thruxton (51°13'N) (01°36'W)	3,000ft	2100	85	270/18	330	12°S	318	5W	323	75	37	29.5
Thruxton	Blackbushe (51°20'N) (00°50'W)	2,500ft	2300	82	290/22	076	8°S	068	5W	073	100	29	17.5
										Total		66	47

From	To	FL/Alt	Safety Alt ft amsl	Tas kt	W/V	Trk T	Drift	Hdg T	Var	Hdg M	GS kt	Dist nm	Time hr/min
Newcastle (55°02'N) (01°41'W)	Carlisle (54°56'N) (02°48'W)	FL60	3500	92	240/25	261	5°S	256	6W	261	69	39	34
Carlisle	Barrow (Walney Island) (54°08'N) (03°16'W)	FL60	4600	91	245/21	199	10°P	209	6W	215	76	51	40
											Total	90	74

	PAPER 1				PAPER 2				PAPER 3				PAPER 4	
1	C	**26**	B	**1**	B	**26**	B	**1**	B	**26**	C	**1**	A	**26**	B
2	A	**27**	A	**2**	A	**27**	B	**2**	A	**27**	B	**2**	B	**27**	A
3	A	**28**	C	**3**	A	**28**	A	**3**	A	**28**	A	**3**	A	**28**	B
4	B	**29**	B	**4**	A	**29**	B	**4**	A	**29**	C	**4**	C	**29**	A
5	C	**30**	B	**5**	C	**30**	A	**5**	C	**30**	A	**5**	B	**30**	B
6	B	**31**	C	**6**	A	**31**	A	**6**	B	**31**	B	**6**	C	**31**	A
7	A	**32**	A	**7**	A	**32**	B	**7**	C	**32**	B	**7**	B	**32**	C
8	B	**33**	B	**8**	A	**33**	A	**8**	A	**33**	B	**8**	A	**33**	A
9	B	**34**	B	**9**	A	**34**	A	**9**	A	**34**	A	**9**	C	**34**	A
10	B	**35**	B	**10**	B	**35**	C	**10**	B	**35**	C	**10**	B	**35**	C
11	B	**36**	A	**11**	C	**36**	B	**11**	C	**36**	B	**11**	A	**36**	A
12	B	**37**	A	**12**	B	**37**	A	**12**	C	**37**	A	**12**	A	**37**	C
13	A	**38**	C	**13**	A	**38**	C	**13**	B	**38**	A	**13**	C	**38**	C
14	C	**39**	B	**14**	A	**39**	A	**14**	A	**39**	C	**14**	B	**39**	A
15	C	**40**	B	**15**	B	**40**	C	**15**	B	**40**	B	**15**	B	**40**	C
16	B	**41**	C	**16**	A	**41**	A	**16**	C	**41**	B	**16**	C	**41**	C
17	A	**42**	C	**17**	A	**42**	C	**17**	B	**42**	A	**17**	C	**42**	B
18	C	**43**	B	**18**	A	**43**	B	**18**	C	**43**	C	**18**	A	**43**	B
19	B	**44**	C	**19**	C	**44**	B	**19**	A	**44**	B	**19**	A	**44**	B
20	B	**45**	B	**20**	C	**45**	A	**20**	B	**45**	C	**20**	C	**45**	A
21	A	**46**	C	**21**	B	**46**	A	**21**	A	**46**	A	**21**	B	**46**	C
22	B	**47**	C	**22**	A	**47**	A	**22**	A	**47**	B	**22**	B	**47**	B
23	C	**48**	C	**23**	B	**48**	B	**23**	C	**48**	C	**23**	A	**48**	A
24	C	**49**	B	**24**	B	**49**	C	**24**	B	**49**	B	**24**	A	**49**	A
25	C	**50**	C	**25**	B	**50**	A	**25**	B	**50**	A	**25**	B	**50**	B

PAPER 1

1	B	11	A
2	C	12	A
3	B	13	C
4	C	14	A
5	B	15	C
6	A	16	B
7	C	17	C
8	C	18	C
9	C	19	B
10	A	20	A

PAPER 2

1	C	11	A
2	B	12	C
3	A	13	A
4	B	14	C
5	C	15	A
6	B	16	A
7	A	17	A
8	A	18	B
9	C	19	A
10	B	20	A

PAPER 3

1	A	11	C
2	B	12	A
3	A	13	B
4	C	14	A
5	B	15	C
6	B	16	B
7	A	17	B
8	C	18	A
9	C	19	C
10	A	20	C

PAPER 4

1	A	11	B
2	A	12	A
3	C	13	A
4	C	14	B
5	B	15	C
6	A	16	A
7	A	17	B
8	A	18	A
9	C	19	B
10	B	20	C

PAPER 5

1	B	11	A
2	C	12	B
3	A	13	C
4	C	14	C
5	C	15	C
6	C	16	C
7	B	17	C
8	A	18	B
9	B	19	A
10	C	20	A

PAPER 6

1	C	11	B
2	B	12	A
3	C	13	A
4	A	14	B
5	A	15	C
6	B	16	C
7	A	17	A
8	C	18	C
9	C	19	B
10	C	20	A

PAPER 7

1	B	11	A
2	C	12	C
3	B	13	A
4	A	14	C
5	C	15	B
6	A	16	A
7	A	17	C
8	B	18	C
9	B	19	B
10	C	20	A

PAPER 8

1	C	11	C
2	B	12	C
3	B	13	C
4	C	14	C
5	B	15	C
6	C	16	C
7	A	17	B
8	C	18	B
9	B	19	C
10	C	20	A

PAPER 9

1	C	11	C
2	A	12	C
3	B	13	A
4	B	14	B
5	A	15	A
6	C	16	A
7	B	17	B
8	A	18	A
9	A	19	A
10	B	20	C

PAPER 10

1	C	11	A
2	A	12	A
3	B	13	B
4	C	14	A
5	C	15	C
6	A	16	C
7	B	17	A
8	C	18	C
9	A	19	A
10	B	20	C

PAPER 1

1	C	11	C
2	B	12	A
3	C	13	B
4	A	14	C
5	C	15	C
6	A	16	B
7	B	17	C
8	C	18	C
9	C		
10	A		

PAPER 2

1	A	11	A
2	A	12	C
3	A	13	A
4	B	14	C
5	A	15	B
6	C	16	B
7	C	17	C
8	A	18	C
9	B		
10	C		

PAPER 3

1	A	11	B
2	C	12	C
3	A	13	A
4	C	14	A
5	C	15	B
6	C	16	C
7	A	17	C
8	B	18	B
9	A		
10	C		

PAPER 4

1	B	11	A
2	C	12	C
3	C	13	C
4	B	14	A
5	C	15	A
6	C	16	C
7	C	17	A
8	B	18	C
9	C		
10	B		

PAPER 5

1	C	11	B
2	A	12	B
3	A	13	B
4	B	14	C
5	C	15	A
6	A	16	C
7	C	17	B
8	C	18	B
9	B		
10	A		

PAPER 6

1	C	11	A
2	B	12	A
3	A	13	C
4	B	14	C
5	C	15	A
6	C	16	B
7	A	17	C
8	C	18	C
9	B		
10	C		

PAPER 7

1	B	11	B
2	A	12	C
3	A	13	B
4	C	14	C
5	C	15	A
6	A	16	B
7	B	17	A
8	C	18	B
9	C		
10	C		

PAPER 8

1	C	11	C
2	B	12	A
3	A	13	C
4	B	14	A
5	C	15	C
6	B	16	A
7	C	17	A
8	A	18	B
9	B		
10	C		

PAPER 9

1	C	11	A
2	C	12	A
3	B	13	B
4	C	14	A
5	C	15	C
6	A	16	B
7	C	17	C
8	C	18	A
9	C		
10	B		

PAPER 10

1	C	11	B
2	B	12	B
3	C	13	A
4	A	14	C
5	B	15	B
6	C	16	C
7	A	17	A
8	C	18	C
9	C		
10	A		

PAPER 1　**19**　"Mayday, Mayday, Mayday; Nottingham radio this is G-DINA a Grumman

AA-5 with a complete engine failure. I intend a forced landing on runway 27 at Nottingham. Presently 2 miles north of the airfield at 2500 feet heading 090. Student pilot (alternatively tyro pilot), one POB."

PAPER 2　**19**　Make the call on 121.5, as you are (should be !) south of 55°N your call is

addressed to 'London Centre' - although this is not essential.

"Pan Pan, Pan Pan, Pan Pan. London Centre this is G-BNHK, a Cessna 152, I am lost on a flight from Luton to Shobdon and I require a position fix. I am at 3000 feet Cotswold QNH 1020 heading 270. I am a student pilot flying solo (alternatively tyro pilot 1 POB). My last known position was overhead Banbury at time 15, I have one hours fuel remaining, I am transponder equipped."

PAPER 3　**19**　"Mayday, Mayday, Mayday. Finningley this is G - BNSP a Slingsby with an

imminent engine failure, intend immediate landing at Finningley. Presently 5 miles west of Finningley at FL55 heading 110, PPL 1 POB"

PAPER 4　**19**　"Mayday, Mayday, Mayday. Biggin Tower this is G-BPZP a Robin DR400. We

have had a bird strike, the canopy is damaged and the aircraft may have other damage. Intend immediate landing runway 03. Presently downwind at 1000 feet on the QFE heading 200. PPL, 2 POB."

PAPER 5　**19**　"Mayday, Mayday, Mayday Southampton approach this is Autoair 03, a Piper

Malibu with a complete engine failure making a forced landing at Beaulieu disused airfield. Current position 1 mile north of Lymington, altitude 1500 feet, heading 340. PPL, 2 POB"

PAPER 6　**19**　"Pan Pan, Pan Pan, Pan Pan, London Information this is G - BNZG, a Piper

Arrow. I have spotted a small boat in difficulties and I intend remaining in present position until assistance arrives. I am presently 10 miles south of the Isle of Wight, altitude 3000 feet in a right-hand orbit, PPL with IMC rating. Request coastguard assistance for the boat, I am presently calculating it's exact position."

PAPER 7　**19**　"Mayday, Mayday, Mayday, Wycombe tower this is G-BXPS. I have

intercepted a Mayday call from G-BNCR, I say again G-BNCR; a PA-28 Warrior with an engine fire, making a forced landing. Its present position is 4 miles south of Thame, altitude 2000 feet heading 270, CPL, 1 POB"

PAPER 8　**19**　"Pan Pan, Pan Pan, Pan Pan. Bristol approach this is G-DASH a Rockwell

Commander with a rough running engine diverting to Bristol airfield. Present position 1 mile west abeam Clevedon, FL50, heading 160. PPL 3 POB"

PAPER 9　**19**　"Pan Pan, Pan Pan, Pan Pan, Liverpool approach this is G-BFLV, Cessna 172

with a seriously ill passenger. Request immediate diversion direct to Liverpool and ambulance on arrival. Presently 4 miles south west of Chester at 2000 feet QNH heading 270, PPL, I have the airfield in sight"

PAPER 10　**19**　"Pan Pan, Pan Pan, Pan Pan, Birmingham approach this is G-BKIS, a TB10

Tobago with a fuel problem, I am returning for an immediate landing at Birmingham. Presently 3 miles east of Sutton Coldfield, altitude 2500 feet in a left-hand turn. PPL, 3 POB, estimate 30 minutes fuel endurance.

Aviation Law Syllabus

AVIATION LAW, FLIGHT RULES AND PROCEDURES

THE AIR NAVIGATION ORDER
Classification of Aircraft

Certificate of Airworthiness to be in Force
Certificate of Registration

Categories - ANO Schedule 3

Limitations of 'Special Category'

Application of Flight/Owner's Manuals and Pilots Operating Handbooks to the Certificate of Airworthiness

Conditions of Maintaining the Validity of the C of A

Requirements for Maintenance Inspections

Certificate of Maintenance Review
Authorisation Sheet

Technical Log

Failure to Comply with the Requirements or Conditions of the C of A

Issue and Renewal of Certificate of Airworthiness
Validity Periods (Calendar Time)

Inspection, Overhaul, Repair, Replacement, and Modification to Aircraft or Equipment

Equipment of Aircraft
Equipment Required in Regulation to the Circumstances of Flight

ANO Schedule

Radio Equipment of Aircraft
ANO Schedule

Certificate of Approval of Aircraft Radio Installation

Flight Radio Operators Licence

Aircraft, Engine and Propeller Log Books
Maintenance and Preservation

Aircraft Weight Schedule
Legal Requirements in Relation to the Certificate of Airworthiness

Grant and Renewal of Licences to Members of Flight Crew
Composition of Crew of Aircraft

Conditions of Issue

The Student Pilot's Privileges and Private Pilot's Licence
Student Pilot Privileges

Medical Certificates

The Private Pilot's Licence
Ground Examinations and Flight Test
Medical Certificate – Renewal

Private Pilot Privileges

Ratings – Conditions of Issue
Privileges of the Aircraft Rating

Additional Ratings

Licences and Ratings – Renewal
Certificate of Test or Experience

In Relation to Description of Flight

Certificate of Test

Certificate of Experience

Period of Validity

Flying Hour Requirements

Personal Flying Log Book
Requirement to Maintain

Personal Details

Particulars of Flights

Recording of Dual, Solo, Cross Country and Instrument Flight Times

Recording of Flight Tests

Instructors Endorsements of Flight Times

Instruction In Flying
Definition of flying Instruction

Requirements for Flying Instruction to be Given

Pilots to Remain at Controls

Pre-Flight Action by Commander of Aircraft
Passenger Briefing by Commander

Dropping Persons or Articles

Carriage of Weapons and Munitions of War

Carriage of Dangerous Goods

Method of Carriage of Persons

Imperilling Safety of Aircraft

Imperilling Safety of Persons or Property
By Intent

By Neglect

Drunkenness in Aircraft
Application to Passengers

Application to flight crew

Smoking in Aircraft
Authority of Commander

Notices in aircraft

Authority of Commander of Aircraft
Legal Requirements to Obey All Lawful Commands

Aviation Law Syllabus

Towing of Gliders
Towing Picking Up and Raising of Persons and Articles

Documents to be Carried
On Domestic Flights
On International Flights

Production of Documents and Records
Requirements of Commander
Requirements of operator
Requirements of Flight Crew
Personal Flying Log Books

Revocations, Suspension or Variation of Certificates, Licences or Other Documents
Whilst Pending Enquiry or After Enquiry
Surrender of Documents
Invalidation of Documents due to Breach of Conditions

Offenses in Relation to Documents and Records
Unauthorised Use of Documents
Alteration, Mutilation or Destruction of Documents or Records
Entries In Log Books or Records
Incorrect Entries (Wilfully or Negligently)
Unauthorised Issue of Certificates
Incorrect Issue of Certificates

Aerodromes – Instruction in flying
The Requirement for Licenced or Government Aerodromes
Permission and Purpose of Use
Aviation Fuel and Aerodromes

Power to Prevent Aircraft Flying

AIR TRAFFIC RULES AND SERVICE

DIVISION OF AIRSPACE IN THE UK

Controlled Airspace
Control Zones
Airways
Terminal Control Areas
Advisory Airspace
Airspace Classifications
Military Aerodrome Traffic Zones

VCM, IMC AND NOTIFICATION
Conditions for VFR Flight
Conditions for IFR Flight
Quadrantal Rule
Semi-Circular Rule
Special VFR Flight

TYPES OF AIR TRAFFIC SERVICE

UNITS
Notams
The UK AIP
Air Traffic Control Centres
Zone Control Units
Approach Control Units
Aerodrome Control Units
Radar Facilities

ALTIMETER SETTING PROCEDURES
Terrain Clearance
Flight Separation
Flight Levels
Transition Level
Transition Layer
Transition Altitude

FLIGHT AT AERODROMES
Aerodrome Traffic Zones
Lights and Pyrotechnic Signals
Ground Signals Used at Civil Aerodromes
Marshalling Signals

FLIGHT PLANS

FLIGHT INFORMATION REGIONS AND SERVICES

FLIGHT IN DIFFERING AIRSPACE CLASSIFICATIONS
Class A
Class A Airways
Class B
Class D & E
Class F & G
Advisory Routes

AIRMISS REPORTING PROCEDURES

AIRSPACE RESTRICTIONS AND HAZARDS
Danger Areas
Prohibited and Restricted Areas
Military Flight Training Areas
Bird Sanctuaries
High Intensity Radio Transmission Areas
Additional Hazards to Aircraft in Flight
Gliding Sites
Free Fall Parachuting Areas
Military Air Exercises
Flying Displays, Air Races etc
Navigation Obstructions

ROYAL FLIGHTS AERODROMES, AGA SECTION OF AIP
Civil Aerodromes
Military Aerodromes
Aerodrome Ground Lights
Identification Beacons
Aerodrome Beacons
Times of Operation

Aviation Law Syllabus

METEOROLOGY

Sources of Information

Requests for Route Forecasts

FACILITATION - Customs and Public Health

Arrival, departure and Transit of civil aircraft on International Flights

Customs Aerodromes

Private Flights - Documentary Requirements

Customs Requirements

Public Health Requirements

SEARCH AND RESCUE

Responsibility and Organisation

Aircraft not Equipped with Radio

Visual Distress and Urgency Signals

Procedures and Signals Employed by Rescue Aircraft

Search and Rescue Regions and Facilities

WARNING SIGNALS TO AIRCRAFT IN FLIGHT

EXTRACTS FROM THE RULES OF THE AIR AND AIR TRAFFIC CONTROL REGULATIONS

Interpretation

Application of Rules to Aircraft

Reporting Hazardous Conditions

Low Flying

Simulated Instrument Flight

Practice Instrument Approaches

Lights or Other Signals to be Shown or Made by Aircraft

Display of Lights by Aircraft
Flying Machines in Flight
Flying Machines on the Ground
Failure of Navigation Lights
Gliders
Free Balloons
Captive Balloons and Kites
Airships

GENERAL FLIGHT RULES

Weather Reports and Forecasts

Rules for Avoiding Aerial Collisions

Aerobatics Manoeuvres

Right Hand Traffic Rule

Notification of Arrival

Flight in Notified Airspace

Choice of IFR or VFR

AERODROME TRAFFIC RULES

Application

Visual Signals

Access to and Movement on the Manoeuvring Area

Right of Way on Ground

Dropping of Tow Ropes

Aerodromes not having ATC Units

Aerodromes having ATC Units

FLIGHT SAFETY

Notifiable Accidents

Flight Safety Bulletin

Accidents to Aircraft on the British Register

AIB Bulletins

AIC's

Meteorology Syllabus

THE ATMOSPHERE
Composition and Structure

The Standard Atmosphere

Pressure, Density and Effect of Altitude Air Density

Altimeter Settings

Altitude

Height

Flight Level

True Altitude

Indicated Altitude

Pressure Altitude

Density Altitude

TEMPERATURE
Adiabatic Cooling and Heating

Stability and Instability

Effect of Dry and Moist Air upon Density

PRESSURE AND WIND
Vertical Motion of the Atmosphere

Horizontal Motion of the Atmosphere

Variations in Surface Wind
Veering and Backing
Diurnal Effects
Land/Sea Breezes
Katabatic Winds
Other Topographical Effects

Wind Gradient/Wind Shear

Flight In Turbulent Conditions
Mountain Waves

FORMATION OF CLOUD AND PRECIPITATION
General Causes of Cloud Formation

Widespread Ascent of an Air Mass

Widespread Irregular Mixing of Air

Local Convective Currents

Local Orographic Disturbances

Precipitation, Rain, Snow and Hail

THUNDERSTORMS AND LINE SQUALLS
Conditions Favourable to Thunderstorm Formation
Frontal Thunderstorm
Pre-Frontal or Line Squall
Air Mass Thunderstorm
Orographic Thunderstorm
Nocturnal Thunderstorm

Development Stages and Cellular Structure
Cumulus Stage
Mature Stage
Dissipating Stage

Effects of Lightning and Turbulence

Avoidance of Flight through or near Thunderstorms

ICE ACCRETION ON AIRCRAFT
Conditions Required for Ice Formation

Types of Airframe Icing

Hoarfrost
Rime Ice
Clear Ice

Effects of Icing upon Aircraft Performance

Precautions, Prevention and Avoidance

Use of De-Icing Equipment
Fluids
Heating Systems
Rubber Membranes

Types of Engine Icing
Precautions/Prevention/Clearance of Carburettor Icing

VISIBILITY
Formation of Fog and Mist

Radiation, Advection and Frontal Fog

Reduced Visibility in Smoke, Rain, Snow, Dust and Sand

Assessment of Probability of Reduced Visibility

Hazards of Flight in Reduced Visibility

DEPRESSIONS AND FRONTS
Air Masses

Formation of Depressions

Formation of Warm and Cold Fronts

Occlusions

Formation of Troughs

Tropical Storms

Hazards of Flight through Depressions and Fronts

Recognition of Deteriorating Weather

ANTICYCLONES
Formation of High Pressure Areas

Ridges and Cols

Flight in Anticyclonic Conditions

FORECASTING AND REPORTING
Observation Instruments

Route Forecasts (inc Visual Weather Service)

Local Area and Airfield Forecasts

Aerodrome Weather Forecasts(TAF's)

Aerodrome Weather Reports(METAR's)

Volmet, Sigmet's and Warnings

The Surface Weather Chart

Navigation Syllabus

FORM OF THE EARTH
Meridians of Longitude and Parallels of Latitude

Great Circles, Small Circles and Rhumb Lines

MAPPING THE EARTHS SURFACE
The Mercator Projection

The Lambert Conformal Conic Projection

The Transverse Mercator Projection

MAGNETIC VARIATION

COMPASS DEVIATION

PRINCIPLES OF NAVIGATION
IAS, RAS and TAS

Wind, Heading and Groundspeed

Calculation of Heading and Groundspeed

The Triangle of Velocities

Dead Reckoning

MAPS AND CHARTS
Types and Scale of Topographical Charts
Practical Use of 1:1000 000, 1:500 000 and 1:250 000 series
Importance of Using Current Charts
Chart Scale

Measurement of Distances and Heights
Units of Distance
Units of Height

Measurement of Angles, Tracks and Bearings

Relationship to True, Magnetic and Compass North

MAP REFERENCE INFORMATION
Chart Series Numbers (Codes)

Latitude and Longitude

Isogonals

Topography
Relief
Hydrographic Features
Cultural Features

Aeronautical Symbols

Aeronautical Information

Conversion of Units (Distance and Height)

MAP READING
Map Analysis

Permanent Features
Relief
Line Features
Spot Features
Unique or Special Features

Features Subject to Change
Water
Other

Effects of Seasons

PREPARATION
Checkpoint Features and Selection

Folding the Map for Use

METHODS OF MAP READING
Map Orientation

Anticipation of Checkpoints
With Continuous Visual Contact
With Restricted Visual Contact
When Uncertain of Position

THE NAVIGATION COMPUTER
Problems Involving the Triangle of Velocities

Determination of:
True Airspeed
Heading and Ground Speed
Track and Drift Angle
Wind Velocity

The Circular Slide Rule
Time, Speed and Distance Problems
Conversion Calculations
Fuel Calculations
Pressure, Density and True Altitude Calculations

FLIGHT PLANNING
Selection of Charts

Plotting of Route

Selection of Altitude and/or Flight Levels (including Safety Altitude)

Selection of Alternate Airfields

Use of UK AIP

Regulated Airspace Procedures

Entry/Exit Lane Procedures

Chart of UK Airspace Restrictions
Danger areas
Prohibited and Restricted Airspace
Military Flight Training Areas
Bird Sanctuaries
High Intensity Radio Transmission Areas

Additional Hazards to Aircraft in Flight

Notams, and Aeronautical Information Bulletins

AIC's

Local Time and UTC

Flight Plan

WEATHER FORECASTS AND REPORTS
The Aviation Weather Forecasting Service
Area Forecasts
Route Forecasts
Aerodrome Forecasts and Reports
VHF Weather Reports

Minimum Weather Conditions Acceptable to Safety

PRACTICAL NAVIGATION
Compilation of the Flight Log
Measurement of Tracks
Determining Safety Altitudes
IAS, RAS and TAS
Computing Heading, True and Magnetic
Groundspeed, Distance and Time

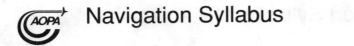

Navigation Syllabus

Selection of Checkpoints, Time Distance
Marks
Fuel Consumption and Total Fuel
Required
Compass Heading, Use of Compass
Deviation Card
Care in Stowing Metal Articles in the
Vicinity of the Compass

Organisation of 'In-Flight' Workload

Completion of the Flight Log

Departure Procedures
Estimated Time(s) of Arrival
Setting Heading Procedures
Altimeter Setting Procedures

Maintenance of Altitude and Heading

Establishing Position

Revisions to Heading and ETA
The 1:60 Method of Heading Correction
The 'Closing Angle' Method of Heading
Correction
Use of 5° and 10° Drift Lines
Revising ETA's

En-Route Checks

Log Keeping

Procedures at Turning Points

In-Flight Procedure to Reach Alternate
Airfields

Uncertainty of Position Procedure
Use of VDF

Lost Procedure

Arrival Procedures
Altimeter Setting and ATC Liaison
Refuelling
Booking In

Aircraft General Syllabus

PRINCIPLES OF FLIGHT

PHYSICS AND MECHANICS REVISION

Speed, Velocity and Force

Pressure
Bernoulli's Principle

Vectors and Moments

Action and Reaction

Work, Power and Energy
Power
Energy

Mass, Momentum and Acceleration

Motion of a Body Moving Along a Curved Path

Force Coefficients

AEROFOILS, LIFT AND DRAG

Air Resistance and Air Density

Aerofoil Shapes

Wing Plan Forms

Lift and Drag
Angle of Attack
Airspeed

Distribution of Lift
Centre of Pressure

Drag - Parasite and Induced
Skin Friction Drag
Interference Drag
Induced Drag

Lift/Drag Ratio

Aspect Ratio

FLYING CONTROLS

The Three Axes

Planes of Movement
Operation of the Elevators, Ailerons and Rudder

Elevators

Ailerons

Rudder

Mass Balance

Aerodynamic Balance

Trimming Controls

Flaps
Simple
Split
Slotted
Fowler

Slats, Fixed Slots, Spoilers and Wing Washout

EQUILIBRIUM

Relationship of the Four Forces

The Forces in the Climb

The Forces in the Descent

STABILITY

Static Stability

Dynamic Stability

Longitudinal Stability

Relationship of C of G to Control in Pitch

Lateral and Directional Stability

Inter-Relationship of Lateral and Directional Stability

THE STALL

Stalling Angle

Wing Loading

THE SPIN

Causes of a Spin

Autorotation

Spin Characteristics

Effect of the C of G on Spinning Characteristics

Effect of Aircraft Inertia upon Spin Recovery Characteristics

TURNING FLIGHT

The Forces in the Turn

LOAD FACTOR AND MANOEUVRES

Effect on Stalling Speed

Structural Considerations

In-Flight Precautions

THE PROPELLER

Construction and Shape

Principles of Propeller Thrust

Lift, Drag, Thrust and Torque

Variable (Controllable) Pitch Propeller
The Constant Speed Unit (CSU)

AIRCRAFT PERFORMANCE

Power Curves
Effect of Aircraft Configuration
Effect of Temperature and Density
Range and Endurance

Climbing Performance
Rate of Climb
Angle of Climb

Take-off and Landing Performance
Take-off Run Available
Take-off Distance Available
Emergency Distance Available
Landing Distance Available

The Take off and Initial Climb - Performance
Effect of:
Wind
Weight
Pressure, Altitude, Temperature and Density

Use of Flaps

Ground and Gradient

The Approach and Landing - Performance
Effect of:
Wind
Wind Shear
Pressure, Altitude, Temperature and Density

Aircraft General Syllabus

Use of Flaps
Ground Surface and Gradient
Ground Effect

WEIGHT AND BALANCE

Limitations on Aircraft Weight
Limits in Relation to Aircraft Balance
Weight and Centre of Gravity Calculations
Weight and Balance in Relation to Aircraft
Category

AIRFRAMES AND AERO ENGINES

AIRCRAFT STRUCTURE

Airframe Structure
Stresses
Fuselage Construction
The Tail Unit
Ailerons, Elevators and Rudder
Trimming Controls
Control Systems
Flaps
Landing Gear
Brake Systems
Aircraft Tyres
Wear
Bulges
Cuts and Scores
Aircraft Seats
Baggage - Stowage and Maximum
Weights Allowed
Control Locks - Types and Purpose

THE FOUR STROKE CYCLE

Valve Timing

IGNITION SYSTEMS

Principles
Magnetos
Ignition Switches

CARBURATION

Carburation Principles
Idling Jets
Accelerator Pump
Idle Cut-Off Valve
Mixture Control System
Fuel Injection Systems
Detonation and Pre-Ignition

CARBURETTOR ICING

Impact Ice
Fuel Ice
Throttle Ice
Recognition
Remedial Actions
Types and Effects of Carburettor Heating

Systems

OIL SYSTEMS

Properties of Oil
Lubrication Methods
Pumps, Sumps and Filters
Typical Systems
Recognition of Oil System Malfunction

FUEL SYSTEMS

Fuel Tanks
Fuel Distribution
Fuel Selection Methods
Fuel Pumps (Mechanical and Electrical)
Fuel Grades and Colouring
Fuel Grades
Inspection for Contamination and
Condensation
Fuel Strainers and Drains
Recognition of
Malfunction/Mismanagement Fuel System
Fuel System Malfunction
Fuel System Mismanagement

COOLING SYSTEMS

The Purpose of Cooling Systems
Methods of Cooling
Operation of the Air Cooling System

VACUUM SYSTEM

Suction Pump
Components of the Vacuum System
Oil Recuperator
Vacuum Regulator
Filter System
Recognition of Malfunction

ELECTRICAL SYSTEM

Types of Fuses
Alternators/Generators
Batteries - Capacity and Charging
Recognition and Procedures in the Event
of Malfunction

VARIABLE PITCH PROPELLER

Handling and Limitations
Ground Checks

ENGINE HANDLING

Ground Considerations
Care of the Propeller
Oil and Cylinder Head Temperatures
Avoidance of Spark Plug Fouling
Induction Air Filter
High Power Operation
Limitations
Inter-Relationship of Engine Instruments
Effect of Mis-use of Controls
Indications of Unsatisfactory Running

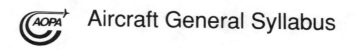

STARTING AND STOPPING

Starting Methods
Float Type Carburettor Engines
Starting In Cold Temperatures
Starting a Hot Engine
Fuel Injection Engines
Starting a Hot Engine

Safety Procedures
Hand Swinging a Propeller
Running Down Methods

AIRWORTHINESS, CERTIFICATION AND MAINTENANCE

AIRCRAFT AIRWORTHINESS

The Certificate of Airworthiness
The Flight Manual
The Flight Manual Supplement
The Certificate of Maintenance Review
The Maintenance Schedule
Pilot Maintenance
Prescribed Repairs or Replacements
Aircraft, Engine and Propeller Logbooks
The Certificate of Release to Service
Pilots Responsibility to Record Defects

AIRCRAFT INSTRUMENTS

FLIGHT INSTRUMENTS

Pitot Static System

THE AIRSPEED INDICATOR

Construction and Function
Calibration and Interpretation of Colour Coding
Errors:
Installation
Density
Compressibility
Pilots Serviceability Checks

ALTIMETER

Simple Pressure Altimeter
Construction and Function
Calibration and Dial Presentations
Effects of Atmospheric Density
Function of the Sub Scale
Errors
Mechanical
Installation
Temperature/Density
Pilot's Serviceability Checks

VERTICAL SPEED INDICATOR

Construction and Function
Errors
Pilot's Serviceability Checks/

GYRO SUPPLY SYSTEMS

Principles of the Gyroscope

TURN AND BALANCE INDICATOR

The Turn Indicator
Construction and Function
The Balance Indicator
Construction and Function
Different Dial Presentations
Pilot's Serviceability Checks

ATTITUDE INDICATOR

Construction and Function
Interpretation of Indications
Different Dial Presentations
Errors and Operating Limitations
Pilot's Serviceability Checks

HEADING INDICATOR

Construction and Function
Use with Magnetic Compass
Errors and Resetting in Flight
Different Dial Presentations
Operating Limits
Caging and Resetting Procedures
Pilot's Serviceability Checks

MAGNETIC COMPASS

Construction and Function
The Earth's Magnetic Field
Magnetic Variation
The Dip Angle
Turning, Acceleration and Deceleration Errors
Magnetism in Aircraft
Deviation and Use of Deviation Cards
Precautions when carrying Magnetic Goods
Pilot's Serviceability Checks

ENGINE INSTRUMENTS

Fuel Indicators (Quantity, Pressure and Flow Meters)
Oil Pressure Indicators
Oil Temperature Indicators
Cylinder Head Temperature Indicators
Exhaust Gas Analysers
Tachometers
Manifold Pressure Gauges
Interpretation of Colour Coding

ANCILLARY INSTRUMENTS

Flap Indicators
Vacuum Gauges
Ammeters and Generator/Alternator Warning Lights
Outside Air Thermometers

FIRE AND SAFETY EQUIPMENT

Fire, Dangers and Precautions

Fire in Flight
Engine/Fuel Fires
Cabin Fires
Electrical Fires
Fire Following a Forced landing

Refuelling Precautions

Description and Use of Fire Extinguishers

Use of Cabin Fire Extinguishers

Hazards of Carrying Flammable Goods

SAFETY EQUIPMENT

Seat Belts and Harnesses

Fire Extinguishers

Life jackets and Life rafts

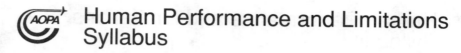

Human Performance and Limitations Syllabus

AEROMEDICAL
Composition of The Atmosphere
The Physical Gas Laws
Basic Physiology and the Effects of Flight

Respiration and Circulation
Oxygen and Effects of Partial Pressure
Hypoxia
Symptoms of oxygen deficiency
Time of useful consciousness
Prevention of hypoxia
Cabin pressurisation
Effects of rapid decompression
Hyperventilation - definition and cause
Symptoms of hyperventilation
Avoidance of hyperventilation
Effects of reduced atmospheric pressure
Effects of acceleration

The Human Senses
The eye and vision in flight
Functional anatomy of the eye
Physiology of vision
Visual Acuity
Limitations of the visual system
The visual vision - scanning techniques
Visual clearing procedures during aircraft operations
Binocular vision
Presbyopia
Visual illusions
Auto-Kinesis
Illusions leading to landing errors
Defective colour vision

Hearing
Functional anatomy of the ear
Inner ear sensations
Effects of altitude change
Noise and hearing loss
Orientation
Sensory illusions and spatial disorientation
Vertigo
Prevention of disorientation

Motion Sickness
Causes of motion sickness
Symptoms and signs of motion sickness
Prevention of motion sickness

Flying and Health
Common ailments
Drugs, medicines and side effects
Alcohol
Drugs
Anti-histamines
Amphetamines
Antibiotics
Anti-hypertensives
Anaesthetics
Drugs of addiction
Precautions
Donation of blood

Fatigue and tiredness
Sleep and fatigue
Precautions against fatigue

The Flightcrew Medical Examination
Standards
Height and weight
Vision
Hearing
Urine analysis
Kidney disease
Diabetes
Blood pressure measurement
The electrocardiogram
Maintenance of personal fitness
Risk factors to health

Passenger Care
Smoking
Adjustment of passenger seats
Use of safety harness or belts
Location, operation of doors and emergency exits
Use of flotation devices
Use of oxygen equipment

Personal Hygiene

Toxic Hazards
Dangerous goods
Carbon Monoxide
Effects and symptoms of carbon monoxide poisoning
Cabin heating systems
Detection of carbon monoxide
Precautions
Avoidance

Incapacitation During Flight

Scuba Diving and Flying

First Aid
Procedures following an accident
Fractured or broken limbs
Severe bleeding
Head injuries
Severe shock
Burns
First aid kit

BASIC AVIATION PSYCHOLOGY

The Human Information Process
Concepts of sensation
Perception
Expectancy/anticipation
Cognitive perception
Central decision channel
Limitation of mental workload
Attention, information sources and stimuli
Memory - types and limitations
Types of memory
Limitations

Stress, management and avoidance
Definition, causes and effects
Concepts of arousal
Environmental stressors
Life stressors
Re-active stressors
Anxiety and its relationship to stress

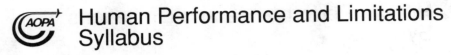

Human Performance and Limitations Syllabus

Effects of stress on human performance

Identifying and reducing stress

Judgement and Decision Making

Types of judgement

Perceptual judgement

Cognitive judgement

Knowledge, skill and experience

Judgement concepts

Attitude development and Risk management

Behavioural aspects

Risk Management

Take-off, approach and landing

Weather related risks

Cockpit management and crew co-ordination

Cockpit ergonomics

Workspace constraints

Cockpit visibility

Mis-interpretation of instruments

Use of colour coded instruments

Aircraft manuals and placards

Use of checklists

An Invitation to Free Membership
of
The Aircraft Owners and Pilots Association

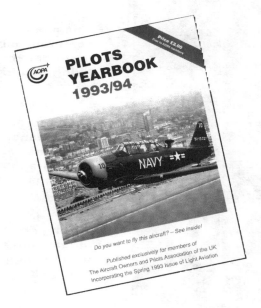

PILOTS YEARBOOK 1993/94

Price £2.00 Free to AOPA members

NAVY

Do you want to fly this aircraft? – See inside!

Published exclusively for members of
The Aircraft Owners and Pilots Association of the UK
Incorporating the Spring 1993 issue of Light Aviation

AOPA's aims

To IMPROVE facilities for General Aviation including the flying clubs and private aircraft owners

To IMPROVE flight safety in all its aspects

To PREVENT unnecessary restrictions on private flying

To CONTROL the costs of private flying

By joining AOPA you become a member of the world's largest pilot's organisation, with branches worldwide. AOPA is owned by its members and represents the interests of pilots and the general aviation community. In the UK it does this through representation and consultation to the CAA, NATS, Government Departments, local government, the Press etc.

As an AOPA member you will receive FREE the quarterly magazine LIGHT AVIATION, and the annual publication, the PILOT'S YEARBOOK. You will also be able to take advantage of special aircraft and pilot insurance schemes, AOPA's legal advice scheme and AOPA conferences and seminars. As if this was not enough, AOPA members can also apply for an AOPA AIRCREW CARD. This identifies you as aircrew at airports and airfields and can be used to help secure discounts at hotels, car hire outlets etc.

It's not often you get something for nothing, and this free membership offer is available exclusively to student pilots. Of course if you are already a qualified pilot you will know of AOPA's work for general aviation. To join AOPA as a qualified pilot just contact them at the address below for membership details - you have nothing to lose but your freedom to fly!

Aircraft Owners And Pilots Association

50a Cambridge Street
London SW1V 4QQ

Telephone: 071-834 5631
Fax: 071-834 8623

To the Membership Department, Aircraft Owners and Pilots Association, 50a Cambridge Street, London SW1V 4QQ.

Name:

Address:

Flying Training Organisation:

I wish to take advantage of free Student Membership until March next year, when I will be invited to upgrade to full Pilot Membership but will be exempt from paying the joining fee of £6.00

However, I wish to receive now:

(Tick box)

☐ My International AOPA Aircrew Card, for which I enclose £10.00

☐ Details of AOPA Wings personal accident insurance scheme

Signature:

Date:

FREE STUDENT MEMBERSHIP

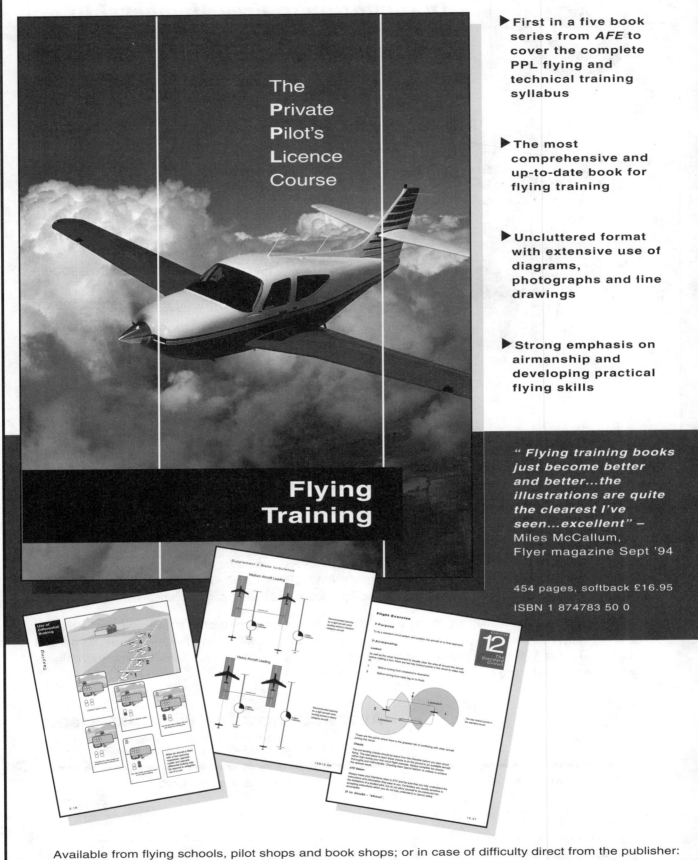